WINGSHOOTING WISDOM
FARM

A Guidebook for Finding & Hunting Public Lands

Ben O. Williams

WILLOW CREEK PRESS

Published by Willow Creek Press
P.O. Box 147, Minocqua, Wisconsin 54548

Library of Congress Cataloging-in-Publication Data:
Williams, Ben O.
  Wingshooting wisdom. Farm : a guidebook for finding &
hunting public lands / Ben O. Williams.
    p. cm.
  ISBN 1-59543-246-9 (softcover : alk. paper)
  1. Pheasant shooting--United States--Guidebooks. 2. Quail
shooting--United States--Guidebooks. 3. Public lands--United
States--Guidebooks. 4. United States--Guidebooks. 5. Ring-
necked pheasant--United States. 6. Northern bobwhite--United
States. I. Title.
  SK325.P5W55 2005
  799.2'46--dc22

                                        2005032794

Printed in Italy

DEDICATION

*To everyone who shares wingshooting endeavors
in the heartland of America.*

ACKNOWLEDGMENTS

I owe a special thanks to Darren Brown, Tom Carpenter, and Barbara Claiborn for their help, and to a host of friends and dogs who have hunted with me over the years.

CONTENTS

Key to Diet Icons

 Cultivated Head Crops: wheat, barley, corn, milo

 Cultivated Green Crops: seeds & greens, alfalfa, clover

 Grass & Sedge: greens & seeds, prairie, pasture, marsh, fescue, etc.

 Forbs: weeds, herbs, tubers, wood sorrels, etc.

 Fruits & Berries: woody plants, nuts, rosehips, strawberry, etc.

 Insects: grasshoppers, ants, beetles, etc.

 Animal matter: snails, frogs, mice, etc.

Key to Habitat Icons

 Grasslands: prairie, pasture, CRP (Conservation Reserve Program)

 Mountains: dense woody cover, shrubby understory, open parks

 Farmland: annual and perennial croplands

 Deserts: washes, arroyos, scrubland environment

 Riparian zones: woody areas along rivers and streams

 Savannas: mixed grass and trees

 Intermountain shrublands: woody brush mixed with grass, sagebrush

 Breaks: steep canyons, gullies, draws

 Forest: conifers, deciduous, cutover forest

 Wetlands: lowlands, marshes

 Homesteads: woodlots, abandoned farmsteads, windbreaks, etc.

 Open water: reservoirs, lakes, ponds

 Foothills: rolling country with draws

Why This Guide Book

The idea for developing a Wingshooting Wisdom Guide Series came to me on two fronts. After many years of hunting across North America, I realized that no helpful step-by-step guide existed that hunters could use to find and hunt a single species of game bird. And being an avid bird hunter, photographer, freelance writer, author of numerous bird hunting books, and a columnist for *Pointing Dog Journal*, I have received hundreds of inquiries from traveling wingshooters who want to know where to go and how to hunt a specific bird.

This series is my response to those queries. Each guidebook will cover several species of game bird that live in close proximity or in similar habitat. The new and fresh ideas you'll find about hunting each bird will help you hunt more effectively whether you're a newcomer or veteran.

But there's much more in this book than just where and how to plan a trip for hunting different species. The first half of the text deals with tactics for hunting each game bird. Each chapter reveals important information about a particular game bird that will help you focus in on which bird you'd like to hunt next. The second half shows you methods for finding the best locations to hunt and for collecting travel information.

Ben O. Williams
Livingston, Montana

FOREWORD

Long gone are the halcyon days when Robert Ruark's Old Man and the Boy could whistle an old bird dog from a shady spot under the porch and stroll to the open fields at the edge of town to put up covey after covey of birds. Times have changed. These days, it's all too easy to sit at home and grouse about shrinking access to private hunting land, hunting grounds lost to leasing, or public land overrun by other hunters or overgrazed by livestock. I used to do quite a bit of this myself to justify why I wasn't heading out to new areas as much as I used to. And it's true—access is shrinking, along with quality habitat in a lot of areas. But it's also an easy trap to fall into, because it's not the whole truth.

The rest of the story is outlined in this series of unconventional guidebooks that not only help you better understand game birds and how they utilize their environment, but also teach you a proven method for locating those elusive birds on hunting trips far from home, where you don't have the luxury of unlimited scouting time. You may find it hard to believe, but the average hunter still can find quality hunting for various game birds across the country, both on public and private land. The proof is in these pages.

Ben Williams has been chasing prairie birds for a very long time and can do so fairly close to home, but he still hits the road each year in search of new hunting country. And he finds it. These places tend to be far from population centers, far from areas that casual hunters with just a few hours to hunt can reach. Many are on public lands or private lands open to hunting through state-run programs, places available to anyone willing to do some homework.

Thomas Edison once said that many people don't recognize opportunity because it's dressed in overalls and looks like hard work. And I think that's the case for a lot of wingshooters today. Finding untrammeled hunting grounds can be difficult, so hunters tend to stay home or find something else to do after the opening weekend of bird season. But it doesn't have to be that way. The method Ben has developed for locating excellent hunting opportunities when local bird populations are at their peak was honed through many years of experience. If you follow this plan closely you will soon be able to zero in on your own new hunting areas, all without killing yourself in the effort or spending huge sums of money.

Hunting trips for the traveling wingshooter should be more than just driving aimlessly down back roads for hours while the dogs whine in the back of the truck and you become increasingly frustrated. Read this book and you'll soon know everything you need to know to make your next trip the best you've ever had, and you'll pick up a wealth of hunting and traveling tips, as well.

—Darren Brown
Editor, *For the Love of a Dog*

As far as appearance and habits go, pheasant and bob-white quail differ greatly.

One was imported from Asia, but thrives here in North America now. He is big, bold, and gaudy, with iridescent plumage incorporating every sheen of the rainbow, and tail-feathers sometimes measured in feet. He runs like the wind, a wily survivor who would rather use his legs than his wings to escape danger.

When he does finally flush, we listen for a cackle or look urgently for those bright feathers, for we shoot only cock birds — plump rockets that weigh a good three pounds or more and burst from cover with a certain racket and a definite defiance.

The other evolved right here in North America, and still survives. He is small, shy and reserved, with brown, tan, buff and cream-colored plumage, and a little bob-tail. He too likes to run, scurrying ahead of our feet and our dogs as he tries to get away. But he is quick to take refuge in a clump of grass or knot of brush in hopes of letting us walk past… a workable plan when you only weigh a half-pound with your crop full.

Although we'd like to shoot only the lighter-faced roosters, hens are also a hunting reality and that's really not a problem. The birds erupt from cover like as many bumblebees all at once, buzzing and fluttering off in every direction of the compass. Then they urgently call back and forth to try and get the covey back together, for there is safety in numbers.

But these great game birds that I've described also offer similarities.

They are each incredibly fun to hunt. Their flushes can unnerve you into making some of the easiest misses of your life! And they inhabit the same kind of countryside — agricultural land where grain fields, pasture, grass and meadow mix with brush, woodlot and wetland, providing a tapestry of food, cover and all-important edges between the two.

"They" are ring-necked pheasants and bob-white quail, and these wonderful game birds form the basis for this edition in the Wingshooting Wisdom series of Bird Hunting Notebooks. With Farm – Ring-Necked Pheasant and Bob-White Quail, it's like having a good friend at your side helping you find a place to hunt, understand the game, locate birds, and identify hunting strategies and techniques.

And I can't think of a better candidate to bring you this information — to take you under his wing, so to speak, and advise you on how to go about approaching your wing-shooting adventure — than my friend Ben Williams.

Ben and his hard-working Brittanys have traveled back and forth across our continent, in pursuit of all our great North American upland birds. He shows that if you're willing to do a little research and planning (a necessary part of any good hunt) and then work some (is there any other way to hunt?), affordable pheasant and bob-white adventures are within easy reach of any upland hunter!

Ben's idea for this book was simple. You don't need to spend a fortune on expensive outfitters, guides or lodges to successfully hunt pheasants and bob-whites. Rather, all you need is a good game plan — a plan outlined concisely in the pages to follow, in Ben's usual clear and descriptive words.

And, true to Ben's form, he has lived the ideas in this book, turning his truck to the nation's heartland for four weeks straight and putting these ideas into action. Simply put, the plan works! It will work for you too.

But, you may ask, who has the time or energy to plan and execute their own bird hunting trip when life is so busy?

You do, when you let Wingshooting Wisdom guide you. It suggests where to start your search for ringnecks and bob-whites. Tells you how to efficiently and effectively plan a trip. Shows you how to secure a hunting spot. Explains where to look for birds, and how to hunt them, once you're there and in the field.

And, with the stories you'll find weaved in, these pages also conjure up the essence of hunting on the classic North American landscape — from quarter-section farmsteads with a covey of quail out in the back forty, to sprawling ranches with the world's wildest ringnecks slinking about out in the riverbottoms, hayfields and irrigation ditches.

While it's true that Ben is partial to his kennel-full of beautiful Brittanys (with a few pointers thrown in for good measure), you'll also discover that he's an "equal opportunity" dog man, and believes there's a place for every breed of dog in the pheasant field and quail pastures … and every reason in the word to take yours along. You'll see how to do it both safely and without hassle.

Whether you've hunted pheasants and bobwhites for decades, or if you're just getting into wingshooting, you need a Bird Hunter's Notebook at your side. Then get ready for the bird hunting adventures of your lifetime.

—Tom Carpenter

❧ ❧

Almost fifteen years ago, I was glancing through a copy of Gray's Sporting Journal when I noticed an upland hunting photo essay by a fellow named Ben O. Williams. As a magazine editor, I like to keep my eyes open for photographers and writers, and so I called my friend David Foster, editor of Gray's, and got Ben's Montana phone number, and he started sending me slides for my magazines.

Shortly after that, in the course of a conversation, Ben invited me out to his home in Livingston for a few days of shooting on Huns and sharptails. I had the time of my life. In the course of that trip, in talking with Ben and hearing his expertise on the habits and hunting of these birds and others, and after seeing his Brittanys work, I asked him about doing some writing. Ben sort of hemmed and hawed a little, but he eventually agreed, and he's been writing ever since, as a contributor and columnist in a number of the best sporting magazines.

And books—a lot of books, this one being the latest.

Ben is nothing if not an experienced traveler, and his specialty is the grail all of us seek: good upland bird hunting on public land. That's what this book is about, and what it will help you do if your mind drifts toward cackling rooster pheasants or the thunderous flushes of coveys of bobwhites. Along the way, Ben gives travel advice, getting your dog from point A to point B, and advice about how to land yourself in the best spots.

Once you get there and find a good place to hunt with good bird populations, how do you go about it? Well, Part I of this book tells you everything you need to know about these great birds – their habitats, their comings and goings, their histories, and – most importantly – how to find them. To those of us from the East, the places that hold good numbers of these birds are big, but Ben shrinks them down for us so we're hunting the productive spots productively.

But if you are going to travel a few miles with Ben Williams by reading this book, you need to know something about him, if you don't already. Ben is an author, photographer, sculptor, architect, and educator. I have shot with him in the high country of the Rockies, in the cornfields of both North and South Dakota, the Southern piney woods, the cactus flats of the desert Southwest, and the moors of Scotland.

Ben feels like dog power is the best solution to finding birds – once you get to where they are. You load up his dogs – no fewer than a half-dozen and usually more – and head for one of his pet stops. Four or five hours later, you're done.

The dogs have all got some work, you've shot enough pointed birds to make it a memorable day, and now it's time to head for the truck.

And all the time you're hunting, Ben's telling you about the birds and the dogs and the places he's been and the grand people he's shot with and traveled with and traded lies with. The conversation alone is worth the trip.

That's what this book is like. I'd guess that the average wingshooter reading it will learn as much or more from it that any book he's ever read. And if you, like a lot of us, spend time on the road traveling to where the birds are, you can't be without it.

—Steve Smith, Editor
The Pointing Dog Journal
The Retriever Journal
The Traveling Wingshooter

RING-NECKED PHEASANT
Phasianus colchicus

Size and Weight
MALE
length: 30-36" (male tail feathers account for 22-23" of total length)
wingspan: 32"
weight: 4-5 pounds

FEMALE
length: 20-26"
wingspan: 24"
weight: 2.5-3 pounds

PART ONE
PHEASANT

Call 'em What You Like

The pheasant is easily the most popular game bird in the United States, although whether or not it is the most hunted "wild" game bird is debatable. But wild or liberated it is still a wonderful and exciting game bird to pursue with or without a dog. The two most common names, ringneck or ring-necked pheasant, are derived from the bird's white neck band. The bird we know is a mixture of races descended from the Caucasian strain of western Asia. Many varieties of pheasants lack this white band. The scientific name for the North America ring-necked pheasant is Phasianus colchicus. Other nicknames include the Chinese pheasant or derogatory names like chink or ditch parrot, but they certainly aren't used by most hunters.

In Flight, in the Hand

If the color of cocks and hens were similar, as with most other game birds, there would be no controversy concerning the shooting of hens. Biological studies show that the average annual mortality of all pheasants, with or without hunting, is about 70 percent. But in most states where pheasant live public support has never favored the harvest of hens. This means that harvesting "wild" pheasants usually

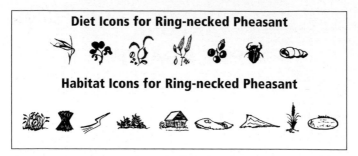

Diet Icons for Ring-necked Pheasant

Habitat Icons for Ring-necked Pheasant

means cock birds only. So learning the difference between male and female is crucial. With a little study it's a simple matter to recognize each sex, not only by color but by size, shape, and sound in flight.

A rooster ring-necked pheasant as the easiest upland game bird to identified in flight. A rooster appears dark in flight compared to a hen pheasant, but under low light or when the bird is backlit both sexes can look very similar. So color alone is not always the best way to identify a pheasant in flight. Other Individual characteristics are the key to mastering quick identification. A male is much larger, with a longer body and tail than a female. And when flushed, the male typically utters a loud coarse cackle: cuck-cuck, cuck-cuck, cuck-cuck. A flushing hen is usually silent or makes a high-pitched sound: queep, queep, queep. An experienced sportsman immediately recognizes a male pheasant in flight and never shoots if there is any doubt.

Pheasants prefer to run rather than fly, but when flushed they're very explosive. Being strong flyers, they can quickly put a lot of distance between themselves and your shotgun.

No other game bird that shares the same habitat resembles a pheasant's characteristics.

In the hand, a rooster ring-necked pheasant is a handsome bird. He's an artist's palette of brilliant colors. The head and neck are metallic blue-green with mixed shades of bright bronze and coppery purple. The sides of the head are vivid red and there is a conspicuous white band around the neck. The body, wings, and legs are a rainbow of colors, ranging from buff and brownish-orange to black. The male is about the size of a barnyard chicken, weighing in at four to five pounds.

The female is as drab as the rooster is gaudy. Her overall general appearance is a mixture of buffs, dusty browns, and mottled grays; she weighs from two and a half to three pounds.

Distribution

At one time, the wild pheasant's range included most of our northern states and the southern edge of Canada. But today much of the bird's habitat has been depleted by human development. Hunting clubs and preserves have sprung up in many areas to give the wingshooter some type of shooting experience. These places use liberated, or released, birds and though enjoyable they won't ever replace hunting wild pheasants. This book doesn't directly address paid hunting, although the subject does come up now and then. The good news is that there are still thousands of acres open to the public that have excellent wild pheasant hunting.

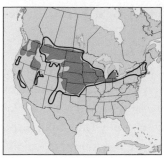

Distribution Map: The red line indicates historical range. There are many gaps within present range due to loss of habitat and human activity.

The pheasant is a bird of farmland areas and cannot survive in a total forest setting. The wide swath between the thirty-eight and fifty-second parallels in the farmland district of North America is the best zone to find wild pheasant. Today the most dependable hunting begins in the midwestern states, starting with portions of Wisconsin and Minnesota and continuing down through Iowa, northern Illinois, northern Missouri, western Kansas, Nebraska, North and South Dakota, and scattered areas throughout the northwestern states all the way to the Pacific coast. Many regions in the West have large agricultural areas created by irrigation or dryland farming practices, and these areas typically host good pheasant populations.

A Bit of History

The Asiatic pheasant was not the first foreign game bird introduced in North America, but it proved the most adaptable, and therefore the most successful, over a large area. In 1881 the first successful planting of ring-necked pheasant occurred in the Willamette Valley in Oregon. The birds did so well that another large shipment was released two years later. Several years later a successful stocking occurred in New Jersey.

After these two successful plantings, it wasn't long before more private individuals and state game departments got involved in releasing pheasants across the nation. A large number of these projects were doomed from the beginning because of a lack of knowledge about wildlife ecology. However, many state game agencies eventually established thriving wild pheasant populations. But it soon became apparent that the corn and wheat belts of the nation were the areas best suited for stable pheasant populations. It's pretty certain that most of the country that can hold pheasants already does. The only exception would be if new irrigated farm areas were established to produce gain crops.

Over the years, the decline of once well established pheasant strongholds is due to a growing human population and the attendant encroachment on good habitat. Urban sprawl and clean farming practices have taken a large toll on pheasant density through the years. But in states where agriculture is the main commodity pheasant populations have continued to do very well. In fact,

Occasionally the Asiatic pheasant comes in a different color phase.

several states have had bumper crops for over a decade, mostly thanks to the Conservation Reserve Program (CRP), which takes former crop and grazing land out of production.

Behavior

Like all game birds, pheasants have different yearly activities. The courtship period runs from late February through March depending on the weather and latitude. As the days lengthen the males begin to crow and fight. Soon after, mating takes place and nesting begins. Whether the male first selects a crowing territory or the female first selects her nesting area is not fully understood.

Once the males' territorial confrontations are over only a single rooster occupies a given "property." Crowing is the rooster's way of showing other males that the location is taken. Usually the crowing area is along the edges of open fields and woody cover. The open cover is usually rather low, such as a cultivated field or grassy meadow. The woody cover may be small woodlot, high brush along an irrigation ditch, a hedgerow, or a swale with good overhead cover. The open cover is used for crowing and courtship display, and breeding most often takes place when the weather is sunny. The dense cover is used for shelter, roosting, and avoiding danger. Mating takes place at least a month after the male courtship activities, and by then the rooster may have collected several other females that have chosen his territory for nesting.

The hen pheasant's primary nesting cover is grass. But similar covers are used if the grass is not of an adequate height to provide an overhead canopy. Pastures, woodlots, and tilled fields don't provide adequate nesting cover and just don't seem conducive to the female's requirements. Heavy grass is more to her liking. Places like irrigation ditches, roadside ditches, edges of shelterbelts, corners of crop fields, and fencerows are utilized before less dense cover. Large clean-farmed cropland areas with little or no edges have had a great impact on pheasant populations. The lack of good nesting habitat is one of the major reasons some areas are void of game birds.

In most geographical areas egg-laying starts in mid to late April and may continue into summer, especially if a nest is destroyed. Most hens will renest if they lose their first clutch and many times will continue until a brood is on the ground or nesting time runs out. The average clutch size is eight to twelve eggs, and it takes about two weeks for the hen to lay this number. Incubation takes roughly another twenty-four days. So it generally takes about five total weeks from the start of laying for the young to hatch, which means that a hen doesn't bring off more than one brood each year. Seeing different size and age groups doesn't indicate that a single hen had more than one brood; rather, it only means she renested after losing her first or second clutch.

A hen's second or three clutch will always have a smaller number of eggs than her first. Many times, more than one hen will lay eggs in a nest, so a larger number will hatch. Whether both hens rear the brood is doubtful, but the one left out will often renest. Sometimes a hen will even drop an

When hunting big roosters most of the credit belongs to the dog.

egg in another game bird's nest, but it won't hatch.

The first broods begin hatching in mid-May. And this is by far the most successful period for good numbers hatched. As the spring season progresses, the success rate declines. Once the last chick hatches, the female leads them all away from the nest. The female rears the brood. Although the male doesn't actually stay with his families, he does play a role in guarding the broods he has fathered from intruders. In the first couple of weeks the chicks are very reclusive and never flush. Their best tactic is simply to freeze. But after two weeks the young chicks can run and fly and they begin to use the best escape route to get away.

The brood spends most of the summer in its nesting territory. At first the chicks' diet is mostly insects, but as the young birds grow they add many other eatable seeds, fruits, and greens to their diet. Young pheasants are notorious for eating anything that moves or grows and fits in their small beaks.

As summer advances, the bird become strong flyers and

are more mobile and less dependent on their nesting territory, especially if food becomes scarce. If food is still available their range expands very little. The family group stays together most of the summer, but as the youngsters grow they begin to show their independence and the family brood starts to break up into a looser group.

As autumn approaches, their summer range may become less adequate and the birds may be forced to shift to new feeding areas. Crops are harvested, hayfields are cut, and the birds' whole habitat may change. Movement is the only way to survive. At this time family groups join up with one another to form larger loose flocks.

There are several facts that all pheasant hunters should be aware of. Instead of being spread more or less evenly over a large range like many other game birds, pheasants tend to concentrate in more restricted cover that suits all their needs during fall and winter. It is not unusual for young pheasants to travel several miles from their summer cover to reach good habitat. Birds often visit grain bins, feedlots, and shelterbelts where food is available on a daily bases. In some areas bird will move down in elevation to valleys or marshy areas with heavy cover.

By late fall, pheasants are strong flyers but cannot sustain extended flights. On flights up to three hundred yards wing action is rapid, with speeds up to thirty-five miles per hour, but during that time they also glide a lot to conserve energy. Pheasants prefer to run under most conditions, but if pushed out of good cover they will flush.

Winter is the critical period for pheasants, yet it still takes severe weather to really cause heavy mortality if food and good shelter are available. The northeast corner of Montana experienced a severe winter storm a year ago. Deep heavy snow covered much on the area. Some efforts were made to feed birds, but that only happened in several places where access was easy. This would be like fertilizing one inch of a football field and hoping the whole playing area would green up. There were reports that many areas had high mortality, but where well-established heavy over-head shelter and native foods were available the birds did quite well. That's why the more "edges" a pheasant lives around, the more likely it is to survive.

Living Requirements

Whether or not you are an experienced hunter, knowing the habits and habitat of a species is an essential part of becoming a knowledgeable hunter. This information helps you understand what to look for in the field and gives you an edge in knowing when and where to find your quarry.

Pheasant requirements vary from day to day and with each season of the year.

Overall the best pheasant populations occur in the northern grain belt of the nation, with corn, wheat, barley, and milo proving most valuable over a long period of time. But a pheasant's food consists of two-thirds vegetable matter and a third animal matter, so agricultural crops alone won't serve birds throughout the year.

Three-fourths of a young chick's diet consists of insects, which are consumed in large numbers as long as available. Adults also eat considerable numbers of insects. Young and old both eat succulent plants, but frequently turn to other foods when they become available. In late summer and fall, pheasants relish all kinds of berries and fruits. When grain becomes available as the

A fine wild ring-necked pheasant rooster.

season advances, birds eat it in large quantities. The next most important foods during the winter are weed seeds, particularly the ragweed and pigweed families and fruits. In fact, if grain is not available weed seeds and dried fruits take its place.

Most of the bird's range provides adequate moisture. They use free-standing water if available, but are able to get water from dew, insects, succulent greens, fruits, and seeds.

Besides food, other daily and seasonal requirements for pheasants include places for roosting, lofting, dusting, and other social behavior.

Edges are vital for winter survival, but they are also the lifelines for a pheasant's year-round activities. Birds frequent cover margins throughout the day, during courtship periods, and when nesting and rearing young. So when you're out hunting, think of the pheasant as a bird of many "edges." As a general rule, more birds are found where two or more different habitats come together.

Despite this wonderful game bird's success in the northern agricultural lands, it has been affected by changing farming practices. The changes from when the bird was first introduced to present day is mirrored by the growing size of farming equipment through the years. At one time, a large plot was twenty acres under cultivation. Today, two thousand acres is considered small in some places.

Pheasants can take advantage of larger agricultural improvements in their environment, but they cannot adapt to a change that is void of food or cover. Without one or the other, the edges become too far apart and are not conducive to the birds' survival. The amount and quality of specific cover types are essential, but the arrangement of this cover is equally important. This is just one reason why CRP has been so helpful in reestablishing good pheasant numbers in some area. Much of the CRP consists of heavy cover adjacent to croplands, creating a balance of cover types and forming more edges.

Three different types of cover are usually required for pheasants to flourish in a local range. These cover types are cropland, grassland, and woody vegetation. There a great variety of tilled agricultural lands in this country, but the best cropland for pheasants is harvested with adequate cover left in the field, such as corn shocks or high wheat stubble. Grass covers a lot of different habitat types. Pasture grass, prairie grass, CPR, grassy swales, grassy strips in cultivated fields, and grassy borders of fields and woodlots are all used in different ways and are helpful for pheasant survival. Woody cover, sometimes called herbaceous vegetation, provides escape cover and winter protection. It also has great value when associated with good feeding areas. Willows, snowberry, cattails, and marshy areas that have high herbaceous vegetation are all useful woody places for pheasants.

One place I hunted for more than twenty-five years had picture-perfect habitat, with all three types of required cover. On any given day you could drive the two-rut bottomland road and see a hundred birds among the patchwork of grainfields scattered the length of the meandering creek. A half-dozen beaver dams flooded the low marshy areas that eventually became choked with bulrushes and cattails. Every oxbow in the creek had a thicket of willows, and patches of chokecherry and snowberries covered the steep hillsides that lifted upward to the angled grainfields above. Fallow earth and wheat stubble covered the four thousand acres of benchland on both sides of the small valley. Grassy gullies and draws snaked through the upper fields, quickly draining rainwater into the creek below.

It was a pheasant hunter's paradise—until the place sold. The old home place became part of a large cattle operation. The new corporate owners drained the beaver dams, cleared out all the underbrush along the creek, seeded the small fields to grassland, and then utilized the entire bottomland for winter pasture and calving. The upper benchland sections were fenced and became large grassland banks used intensely as summer pastures. It wasn't long before this land-use pattern completely eliminated the pheasant population on this parcel, and bird numbers in the surrounding area were also affected.

There have been many changes in the rural landscape through the years. Some of these changes have occurred so gradually that we aren't even aware of them. The small farms of yesteryear provided more pheasant habitat since fields were smaller and had more fencerows, wide corners, and shelterbelts. In other words, there was more cover diversity and more edges. A distribution of food and cover is important in any given area. For instance, twenty acres of good pheasant cover dispersed around a large field are much more useful than good cover concentrated in one place. As large farms grew larger, fences, corners, and shelterbelts were ripped out to provide huge fields for easier cultivation. These large fields soon become void of any heavy cover, and also pheasants.

Today there are still countless areas in rural America that have excellent pheasant habitat. Pheasants are just one small product of an agricultural environment and are mostly associated with croplands, which are usually privately owned. So asking a farmer or rancher not to produce the maximum crop capacity on their land is a bad approach unless they are compensated for game habitat

Pheasants and the Conservation Reserve Program

The land enrolled in CRP has to have permanent cover—grass where grass once grew—and be out of production for a period of ten years. Congress recently reauthorized CRP in a form similar to the last program, although the landowner's annual compensation for each acre enrolled is less than in the old program. Many farmers and ranchers that were in the old program are staying in the new one. New landowners are also enrolling in the revised program.

CRP has created large amounts of upland bird habitat. Never has so much land been put back into grassland in such a short span of time. Large areas of natural grassland have been restored and now provide game birds with good nesting habitat, roosting cover, shelter from predators, and food throughout the year. These grasslands are fenced and rarely used by livestock, making the carryover vegetation in spring ideal for nesting birds. Pheasant populations in many areas have rebounded thanks to CRP.

improvements. Many land owners are genuinely interested in preserving wildlife and are willing to develop habitat areas with help or for a price.

Many federal and state agencies have programs that benefit wildlife and provide shrubs and trees for shelterbelts. For over a decade the federal government has implemented the Conservation Reserve Program. This is a national program that provides incentives to landowners for taking marginal soils out of production and for seeding them to permanent grassland/brushland cover and food plots. Over the years, this program has been a huge boon to pheasants and other

Walking towards two dogs pointing pheasants in a large CRP field. CRP (Conservation Reserve Program) has been a boon for pheasants and has opened up thousands of acres for the traveling wingshooter to hunt.

game birds and has restored thousands of acres of suitable habitat. State agencies have also fostered partnerships with landowners and encouraged them to develop better habitat conditions for wildlife. In return, they are compensated according to the number of hunters using their lands. Many state and federal agencies have restored public lands for upland game birds and other multiple-use purposes, as well.

Hunting Strategies

More people hunt ringnecks than any other upland game bird, and the various hunting methods seem nearly as numerous as the pheasant hunters themselves. But no matter how you pursue this large, wily game bird, success comes more often when you learn to recognize good pheasant cover, know the birds' daily movements and how weather affects them, and formulate a plan of how best to approach a particular parcel of land. Every piece of land is unique and part of the fun is devising a strategy to outwit a smart old rooster that knows every escape route available.

For the local hunter, scouting beforehand is an effective way to find birds before the hunting season starts, but it's not feasible for the traveling wingshooter on a long trip. So it's essential to be able to read pheasant cover and learn how a bird spends it day no matter where you go to hunt. This will save you valuable time in the field, which is critical on any hunting trip.

Food, lots of different levels of cover, and a water source are the basic requirements for wild pheasants everywhere. Learning how pheasants use these combinations is the key to a successful hunt. So when talking about locating good pheasant cover we are generally referring to feeding, breeding, nesting, roosting, escape, travel, and winter cover. The water source requirement is one of the most flexible because birds can also obtain water from succulent greens, fruits, and insects or rain and dew collected on plants during the summer or ice and snow in winter.

We often think of food, moisture, and cover as separate entities, but that's not always the case. Take mature corn, for example. It has all three attributes pheasants need to live. It's not unusual to find pheasants in standing or shocked corn at any time of the day as long as there is good overhead cover. I can remember several occasions as a youth when my springier spaniel refused to leave a cornfield and finally trapped and flushed a cagey old rooster.

Except with fall crops like corn that have not been harvested, most pheasant hunting strategies should be geared toward regular feeding and loafing hours. A good point to remember is that all of these types of cover must be located within a two-mile radius, which is about the average range of a pheasant. These cover combinations must stay intact year-round. If one or more of these various covers are destroyed the local pheasant population will move to better habitat or die off.

It's easy to describe good habitat in writing, although there is no substitute for studying habitat and gathering information firsthand. Reading and/or talking to someone

It's easy to describe good habitat in writing. But a good photo is worth a thousand words. There is no substitute for studying good habitat and gathering information firsthand.

Ring-necked Pheasant Ground Sign

The knowledge of signs on the ground left by a pheasant is very helpful in knowing that they are using an area to feed, roost, or loaf, and can save time in the field when looking for that species.

Tracks: look for tracks in sand, snow, mud and powdered dirt.

Single droppings: look for single droppings in open areas and in grain fields. Droppings are chicken-like in appearance.

Roosting site droppings: birds roost individually, but in the same proximity, called clusters.

Feathers: single feathers can be on the ground, hanging in brush, at watering places and dusting holes

that has spent time in the field pursuing pheasants is also helpful, but experience in the field is the best teacher as long as you make an effort to observe the surroundings and think about why the birds are using that landscape. Record this information in your mind or, better yet, take notes on what good cover looks like. You can then use this as a model when hunting new parcels of land. When I'm in new country I drive from one walk-in area to another and analyze whether the block of cover holds pheasants or any other game birds I happen to be hunting. It doesn't take a genius to figure out good cover for any kind of game bird. But it does take a little effort on your part to learn to read cover combinations, the relationship of edges, and how the overall landscape fits the birds' everyday needs.

Different cover types serve various functions throughout a pheasant's live. Thickets of shrubs, trees, tall CRP fields, and cattail patches provide shelter for shade during hot days in summer and from wind-driven storms during winter. Woody plants with high overhead cover protect pheasants from aerial predators year-round. Field edges and corners, ditches, fencerows, hedgerows, and roadside right-of-ways that are heavily vegetated provide travel lanes and escape routes for pheasants to move freely and undetected between different locations. Nesting cover is more specialized and must include undisturbed vegetation year-round. CRP fields, right-of-ways, shelterbelts, and abandoned farmsteads are a few of the areas that typically have enough grass and weeds to make good nesting cover. Wetlands, CRP fields, grassy draws, and weedy patches are used for roosting and loafing sites. Bulrush sloughs and cattails are favorite pheasant hideouts from ground predators and hunters during the bird season.

An ideal setup for pheasants includes a productive grainfield that can be reached by a short flight or by walking from a high grassy site suitable for roosting. There should be tall weeds or thick brush in between, with a water source close by. In reality, birds often have to move a considerable distance to feed and rest, but the best situa-

Bulrush sloughs and cattails are favorite pheasant hideouts from ground predators and hunters during the bird season.

tion would involve a short distance between feeding and roosting sites.

It's also essential to learn as much as possible about a pheasant's daily movements and feeding habits. What a bird does throughout the day is directly related to the kind of cover available. After roosting all night in a grassy location that usually has some overhead cover, pheasants go to feeding cover at dawn and stay there until about midmorning. From then until early afternoon, these feeding areas will be deserted. So don't waste time hunting feeding areas at this time.

During midday, turn your attention to areas where pheasants loaf, dust, or just hang out. If it's warm, look for an open sunny area with high overhead woody cover that's open underneath so the birds can dust and still see out. Big, overgrown CRP fields are used extensively during midday. These large back-to-grassland fields are ideal places to find noontime pheasants, especially it they're adjacent to grain-fields. I know many pheasant hunters who choose not to hunt these big CRP fields. Their reasoning is usually that the cover is too thick and hard to work. But just looking at a big field from the edge doesn't necessarily give you an overall pic-ture of the entire half or whole section of land. I know of no big fields that have the same cover throughout their entirety.

There is a half section (320 acres) on one of the national grasslands that I've hunted for years. If you just look at it from the edge the tall grass seems impossible to walk through or for a dog to work. But in the center there is a large, long draw and along the sides there are patches of prickly lettuce that are like a banquet to prairie chickens and sharp-tailed grouse.

Big, sterile-looking CRP fields need to be explored, so don't overlook these areas. A couple of years ago I was walk-ing the edge of a big walk-in CRP field for bobwhite quail when two of my Brittanys got side-tracked and started working pheasants. I was after quail, though, so with some effort I finally got my dogs off the running pheasants. When we got to the end of the fencerow about twenty pheasants blew out of the end of the field and settled in a long patch of cattails. My partner wanted to go after them, but I declined because I didn't want my pointing dogs dis-tracted by pheasants while hunting bobwhites.

When walking, look for telltale bird signs such as feathers, droppings, and dusting places. If you find them it's easy to determine how fresh they are, and the cover will tell you what time of day the birds are using the area.

Most years I hunt a few new and different locations for pheasants. I enjoy being in new country and studying the lay of land, the habitat, and how best to find the birds. Last season I took a trip to Kansas and hunted the walk-in areas open to the public. Most areas were half or full sections of CRP, and I must say, they were a blast to hunt. Not only were they productive, but I had little, if any, competition from other hunters.

Be aware of the weather and weather forecast for the areas you hunt. Weather influences the choice of cover used by pheasants. Bird feeding activities change in cold or stormy conditions, and they may not leave their roost sites until late morning. As the days become shorter, they spend more time feeding.

Before I went to Kansas I did my homework and made sure the information I received about the best time to go was correct. This information included notes on the weather and, more importantly, when the fields were most likely to be void of other pheasant hunters. In most areas, I have found that the majority of pheasant hunters only go out two to three times per season, usually on early weekends during the season. So opening day is not the best time for the traveling pheasant to be afield. My advice to anyone planning a pheasant trip to an unfamiliar place is to go later in the season, even if you have to hunt birds in the snow. If fact, I think that hunting pheasants with snow on the ground is ideal. And later in the season many birds that have been hunted over become pretty smart, making it lot more fun. Finally, going later almost always ensures that you have good hunting areas to yourself.

When you shoot your first bird in a new area, stop to examine its crop to see what local birds are eating. This may help you determine the feeding location of the birds, an area you can return to on subsequent trips. I have had wonderful hunting luck after taking a crop sample from any kind of game bird I hunt. I can assure you it will pay dividends.

About Dogs

Pheasant hunting can be a Sunday social event with carloads of hunters or a solitary sport. It's a gun sport for young and old and the hunting methods vary according to the type and size of the cover available. Pheasants can be hunted without a dog, but it's certainly not as effective as having a canine companion along, unless you're with a large group of hunters. Large parties can have good success without dogs by having some hunters walk a large area while others stand as blockers at the end of the field. In fact, many cornfield hunters who use the drive-and-block method consider any dog a nuisance except for retrieving. But hunting with a large group or with or without a dog is a personal preference.

My advice for the lone hunter with no dog is to choose small covers, such as narrow swales, overgrown corners of fields, fencerows, little creek bottoms, small fields, and cat-tail patches. The key is to go slow and walk in a zigzag pattern, pausing occasionally to give the birds time to get nervous that they've been spotted. Hit every thick patch a couple of times from different directions and give every likely hiding place a kick or two.

Relatively small patches of cover are great places to find a single bird. First slowly walk completely around the perimeter. Tighten the circles as you continue around and the bird will eventually flush as you come to the middle. Or try backtracking a fencerow; many times this helps to unglue a wily old bird.

Overall, pheasant hunting without a dog is difficult because the birds can outrun any walking hunter. This guidebook is intended to help everyone find a place to hunt pheasants, but it's mainly geared toward the traveling wing-shooter who has a bird dog and hunts alone or maybe with one or two buddies. I've done a lot of pheasant hunting alone, and I enjoy it immensely. Since I was a kid I've always had and loved hunting dogs, and they have always been part of my hunting experience. I believe any dog is better than no dog at all for finding game birds, and certainly for locating them after the shot.

A lot of hunters have dogs they use exclusively for pheasants, and I'm sure they get a lot of birds with them. But the fact is, no dog has ever been breed just for pheasants.

At one time many hunters categorized certain gun dogs according to a species of game bird. There were ruffed grouse dogs, bobwhite quail dogs, duck dogs, and so on. Traditional ruffed grouse hunters are mostly English setter folks, don't hunt in crowds, and have secret coverts they only pass down to kin. Southern bobwhite quail hunters are a social group, use high-tailed pointers, and "shoot" but do not "hunt." But no one ever linked an individual canine breed to pheasants, in part because they lack the long tradition of certain native game birds.

The only native game bird that fits the same description as the pheasant is the prairie chicken, which was more a "working man's bird" than a member of the American elite of game birds. These days, the pheasant has largely replaced the chicken as the game bird of the people. Chickens and pheasants have always been hunted much the same way.

A good pheasant dog is cautious and works the cover methodically.

The method of taking, the make of shotgun, and the kind of dog were never important issues when hunting either of these birds. Early on, folks that pursued chickens were meat hunters, and putting food on the table was the main objective. A specialized dog for this type of hunting never existed. The same holds true for modern pheasant hunting. The closest we have to a true pheasant dog these days would probably be one of the flushing breeds. And I would bet my last nickel that more pheasant hunters use a Labrador or golden retriever than any other breeds.

I have hunted pheasants with just about every kind of bird dog there is, but if I were to hunt pheasants exclusively I'd join the brigade of Labrador owners. Labs are brush-busting machines that love hunting heavy cover, and they do an excellent job of plowing through the thick stuff where pheasant like to go. These big dogs have the physical and mental capacity to get the birds in the air and are particularly effective at rousting out big roosters. Labs are easily trained and anxious to please their owners, but need to hunt close enough for the hunter to get good flushing shots. Another advantage a Lab has over many other dogs is its short hair, which is easy to care for after the hunt.

You could also make a case that the springer spaniel and English cocker are the best breeds for the serious pheasant hunter. They work close in front of the gun and are good retrievers. Some are a bit small for fetching a big rooster, but I won't hold that against them, for they certainly have big hearts.

Years ago I even hunted with a couple of good beagles that worked running pheasant like two pros. One dog would circle and pinch the bird into flushing. But most hounds aren't usually thought of as pheasant dogs.

Personally, I'd just as soon not hunt pheasants with my current kennel full of Brittanys or pointers. But I still do on occasion, usually with my older, more experienced dogs that have slowed down some. For many years I hunted pheasants religiously every weekend during the season. But over the years I developed a line of Brittanys to run bigger than other pointing breeds in order to cover the big open prairie country I most often hunt. Open country pointing dogs, or for that matter, any big running dog, just aren't the best choice for hunting running pheasants in heavy cover.

Several pointing breeds have a reputation for hunting close, and all of these breeds include some excellent pheasant dogs. They are typically cautious and work the cover methodically. Don't blame pointing dogs that don't hunt close, though, they're just doing what they have been bred to do.

A dog doesn't have to be genius to hunt pheasants. If fact, it doesn't even have to be a recognized breed. One of the best dogs I ever hunted pheasants over was a mixed-breed farm dog. When I would stop and ask the landowner for permission to hunt the dog would come along, many times outperforming my dogs. She knew just how to trap a running pheasant. So as long as your dog loves to hunt pheasants, the breed doesn't really matter too much.

I like to hunt with only one other person when pursuing pheasants. And for the traveling wingshooter one partner and a couple of dogs is an ideal combination. Let me explain. A dog or two on the ground can cover more ground than a platoon of pheasant hunters. Two hunters with dogs can walk both side of a fencerow or spread out in a crop or CRP field and cover a wide area with the dogs working in between. Another good method is to separate and work opposite ends of a field, all the while walking toward one other. This is extremely affective when hunting a big CRP field or a long line of cattails. A good tactic when hunting along a riparian zone or man-made waterway that meanders or has oxbows is to pinch the pheasants against the water's edge, which closes off the covered escape route.

A high creek bank with brush below is a good place to trap a wily rooster into flushing.

No matter what strategies you use, the most one important approach for hunting pheasants is to go slow and let the dogs work all the cover. Pheasants become very nervous when a hunter walks slowly or pauses to wait for the dog to finish its job.

Where to Go

Over the last ten years, the outlook for pheasant has been very promising thanks to expanding CRP fields throughout the Great Plains. North Dakota, South Dakota, Nebraska, Kansas, and Montana all have excellent public lands to hunt. Indian reservations and private lands administered by state game agencies are also open to the public for hunting game birds. Parts of Oregon, Washington, Idaho, Oklahoma, and Wyoming also have had excellent hunting the past few years. With CRP intact for the foreseeable future, the overall pheasant population looks good for some time to come.

I Figured Them Out

Years ago I had two Brittanys named Gina and Lola. Gina was as good a bird finder as Lola was bad. But when Lola pointed you were guaranteed a bird close by. And if it was a rooster, her nose would be in the shadow of the pheasant's tail. Though poor at finding prairie game birds, her forte was pointing pheasant that hunkered down or stopped where the cover ran out. Lola would not be consisted a big-running Brittany by today's standards because her method was methodical, but she'd certainly be considered a pheasant hunting genius for her ability to root out the cagiest of roosters.

There are times and places where pheasants follow exactly the some routine day after day. I've known of few such areas over the years, but the best setup I had for several seasons was fairly close to town. I could teach at the high school all day and still have time to hunt there before dark.

Each morning and late afternoon the birds traveled to and from their feeding area. But it seemed to be easier to catch them off-guard in early evening. The reason was that during their morning trip the pheasants had plenty of time so getting back to their loafing area was more leisurely. Nailing down exactly when the birds would be in the weedy draw was difficult during the morning. But their late afternoon feeding session forced them to hurry back before darkness fell, making them more predictable. My strategy worked perfectly at this time because the birds had no alternate escape routes.

A cut hay meadow surrounded most of the forty acre food patch, and there was a wide, deep draw full of willows at the river's edge where the pheasants lofted midday. Alongside the willow patch, a large grassy field provided roosting cover at night. The willows continued up the draw for a hundred yards then gave way to drier vegetation like buck brush and various weeds. The draw narrowed through the hay meadow, then stopped abruptly at the border of the grainfield. From the lofting area, the pheasant would move up the brushy draw around three o'clock and arrive in the open grainfield by four, returning by the same route to their roosting site before dark.

Once the birds started to feed they would fan out into the grainfield and become very wary because they were so visible. If they saw any vehicle or object moving toward them they would take off and fly back to the safety of the willow thicket. Both the grainfield and the willow thicket were impossible for the dogs to hunt, but if I timed it right I could trap the birds in the heavy cover of the draw. The trick was to be there when the birds where out of sight in the weedy draw during their transition period. Once they were in the draw they couldn't see me coming.

I hunted it once this year and the vegetation in the draw and the crop field hasn't changed, so the plan is the same as it has been for the past four years. Only an abrupt change in the weather can foul up the timing. The only caveat is that the area can't be hunted too often. At most, I only it hunt once during a week and never on weekends, for it only takes an hour to cover the draw. Any pheasant population that has the same routine day after day can't pressured much. Once a week or, better yet, once every two weeks is about the limit before they get wise and change their feeding pattern.

Midafternoon. Not a cloud in the sky or a breath of wind. The sun is low over the southern hemisphere. The temperature is 45 degrees and falling. The plan today is to do exactly what my hunting partner and I did ten days ago. The last time we both got our two-bird limit, but that doesn't happen often. Usually one or the other of us gets most of the shooting because the birds are being pushed in one direction.

I drop off a fellow teacher by the name of Brad, a faithful hunting companion and a superb wingshooter, and my dog, Gina, on an idle dirt road that bisects the lower end of the draw, within a stone's throw of the Yellowstone River. Then I backtrack in a large circle and park at the other end of the draw along the grain field. The stubble is cut low enough so that I can see if any birds are feeding in the field.

While I'm surveying the area with my 10x40 binoculars, two hen pheasants flush from the center of the field and fly high overhead back toward the river. I decide that our timing is perfect, as I've often observed hens feeding first before any rooster sets foot in the open field. I can't prove this, but it seems that the males use the hens as a safeguard against unforeseen danger. Or perhaps because they're so drab in color they are less concerned about being spotted in the open. Neither of these suppositions is backed by scientific study, but it's food for thought.

Lola knows the full routine and by the time the little blue Volkswagen has stopped she is pushing her nose against the back window, eager to get out.

Partly closing the car door, I say, "Lola, sit," as I pull the 20 gauge over-under out of its case. I put my vest on next, and Lola barges out the door, knowing I'm ready to go. Meticulously working the head of the draw, she pays no attention to three hen pheasants that flush farther ahead.

"Slow down," I command, as Lola accelerates while ground trailing pheasant scent down the weedy draw. Then a single shot rings out and I figure the roosters are already moving along the draw toward my hunting partner. Another shot echoes from the same direction and Lola and I quicken our pace toward the willow-covered roosting site. Gina must be doing her job, for she is a master at stopping pheasants running toward her. Somehow she's figured out how to cut them off before they get around her.

A third shot thunders far down the draw, and I'm wondering if Brad got into a covey of Huns along with a few roosters. He rarely misses a big rooster, but Huns normally don't frequent the heavy weedy cover this time of day. So something unusual must be going on. To my amazement, a fourth and fifth shot ring out. Following the sound of Brad's light 12-gauge side-by-side, I spot white specks coming toward me. The puzzle is solved; a large flock a sharp-tailed grouse passes high overhead out of shooting range. I watch them fly hell-bent for the hills. Then I hear another shot much closer and small bunch of sharptails comes over lower. But I hold up from shooting and don't watch these birds fly off because Lola is pushing hard on scent.

She soon stops dead in her tracks. Her head and body are low to the ground, telling me she has penned down a pheasant. I move into the wind toward the dog, then take two steps to the side and stop. Lola dives into the heavy buck brush. I'm ready because I'm sure she has a pheasant. But nothing happens. Looking beyond her point I see two hens and a rooster flush fifty yards ahead. "Good dog, Lola," I called out, but she is still hot on the trail of more birds. She points again and a suddenly pheasants fill the sky, all going in Brad's direction. But I hear no report from his shotgun. Then all is silent.

Lola continues working the brush until she sees Gina coming and runs to meet her. Minutes later Brad arrives with a grin you can see for a mile.

"I didn't hear you shoot. What happened?" Brad asks.

"I didn't get one bird in range to shoot. They all flushed your way. I did see a big bunch of sharptail wing by and heard you shoot several times. How did you do?" I ask.

Brad pulls out two rooster pheasants, two sharp-tailed grouse, and two Huns. Laughing, he says, "Your dog Gina got 'em all. She pointed the sharptails in the bottom feeding on roschips. The Huns were on the edge of the cut field. She could see them when she pointed, but they held like glue. And she stopped the running pheasants in their tracks. You know, Ben, this may be the best hunting and dog work I've had in years."

"I believe we can do it several more times this year," I said. "There are still plenty of roosters around."

Two years later, the ranch got sold. The lower draw became a feedlot for holding cattle before shipping. The willows disappeared along with the grassy pasture and the upper forty acres is now part of the cut hay meadow. The pheasant are gone, but I continue to hunt the upper hills for Huns and sharptails. And when I do, I look down toward the river where I used to hunt pheasants and think about the good times I had with my friend and those two dogs.

Long Tails and Ivory Spurs

Depending on the weather, the late season can be the best time to use a pointing dog on pheasants if circumstances are favorable. The conditions on the ground dictate how the pheasants react. If there are several inches of snow the whole playing field changes for a pointing dog. Pheasants prefer not to plow through snow if it gets too deep, so this can be a wonderful time to hunt them because they're no longer footloose track stars.

The landscape becomes surreal, and tracks in the snow offer visible proof of the magic of a pointing dog's ability to find pheasants. When the dog points and the tracks stop at a clump of cover the hunter can almost smell what's going through the dog's nose. And both dog and hunter share that special moment just before the bird launches from its hiding place. Fresh snow is a blueprint of what the bird has been doing, and a clue to where it's going next. New snow negates a pheasant's usual game of hide-and-seek. They become more vulnerable if they're being followed.

I've been fortunate enough to hunt pheasants on numerous days with a skiff of snow underfoot, but not many when a fresh blanket covers the ground. I've come to realize just how memorable these events can be, and I know they don't come along often.

After a large breakfast of biscuits and gravy and what

seemed like a gallon of coffee, Bill and I drive south, kicking up a cloud of new fallen snow.

Four to five inches of power fell during the night, adding a coat of shimmering whiteness to the landscape. But it is still easy to distinguish the field corn from the grassy swale that runs through it. Occasionally the crop does poorly and is cut for silage, leaving the field void of vegetation and no cover for the birds. But this year the corn grew tall and matured strong and after being harvested the field is lined with rows of bent corn stalks and a wealth of weeds.

The cornfield is framed on three sides by decaying spilt-rail posts and a decrepit sheep wire fence. The fencerow is clogged with wild plum and chokecherry thickets and other woody plants compete for space. Weeds and herbs continuously encroach on the field. On the far end the land dips to form a large marshy lowland bog full of swamp grass, sedges, and cattails. Beyond lies a quarter section of high woodlands. The whole setting is a perfect mix of food and cover for wild game, especially pheasants.

As soon as I arrived in the pickup the birds hoofed it to the end of the cornfield, never even stopping at the marsh, and disappeared into the woods—smart late-season veterans.

The place has been a family farm for years, but Bill Clay had no desire to become a farmer and moved on. His father worked the farm alone and eked out a living for years and when he got too old to continue he leased the tillable ground to a neighbor. When the old man died Bill inherited the place. He rented the house and continued to lease the crop-land with the understanding that it be kept wildlife friendly for hunting. Bill is mostly a deer hunter and has never had a bird dog, but he loves mine and goes pheasant hunting with me when he can. He usually tries to block the birds at the far end of the field, but this late in the season the birds definitely have the advantage. At least until it snows.

A windless, cloudless December day is not unusual for this time of year. I put down Mac and Pat, two of my Brittanys, and their breathing pumps warm mist into the crisp, cold air. Bill and I walk past the large red barn, its two large open doors revealing weeds and windblown dirt. They show no sign of being closed for years. A Farmall tractor that matches the color of the barn looks tired from years of use. I stop to check its vintage. The letter "H" tells me it's a much larger tractor than the one I drove to collect the corn my family picked by hand when I was a kid. Bill stands out-side the old building with his shotgun over his shoulder watching for any wildlife movement.

The two dogs are already kicking up snow halfway down the fencerow by the time we round the corner of the barn and enter the cornfield. I call Mac and Pat back before they get out of sight. Snow covers the shucked husks and the bent cornstalks form a canopy of cover. Each one is a poten-tial hiding place for a colorful pheasant to stay dry and keep out of sight. As we walk the cornfield toward the lowland marshy bog the dogs work along the edge of the fence line. Halfway into the field I spy a single pheasant track between a row of cornstalks. I wonder how far the bird might walk before it stops.

Then Bill calls out, "Pheasant tracks, Ben."

I call the dogs over and they plow through the snow in front of me and freeze like two ice sculptures. In a low voice I whisper to the dogs, "Easy, easy now," then signal to Bill that there are birds ahead. Slowly the dogs move up and then stop for us to catch up. Two sets of tracks lead down the row I'm walking.

The new snow makes tracking easy and it's interesting to see how the dogs work the bird scent. My eyes scan ahead to see if any tracks have disappeared under the cornstalk cover. I lose both sets of prints for a moment and then spot them in the next row, converging with the tracks Bill's been following. Both dogs stop abruptly, side by side and almost touching, and again wait for us to catch up.

"Ben," Bill says softly, "all three sets of tracks have disappeared under the cornstalks."

"There are no tracks coming out my side," I answer.

The dogs stay motionless as I slowly walk past them. Gun ready, I slide my hand above the forearm and feel the safety under my glove. I look over at Bill, and then nod my head. He walks in without hurrying, kicking each cornstalk as he goes. I watch the two Brittanys; they roll their eyes but never move a muscle.

"Trust me, Bill," I say, "the birds didn't run out this side so they're in there somewhere."

Bill stops and turns toward me. Just then a rooster and

Bill stops and turns toward me. He is looking right at a big rooster. He fires, making a clean kill.

hen flush ten yards out. There is no need for him to spin around. He is looking right at the big rooster. He fires, making a clean kill, and feathers drift slowly down to earth. He turns back, waiting for the third bird to flush. The sound of beating wings bursts through the cornstalks and a big rooster flushes on my side but out of range. Another hen flushes unexpectedly as Mac crosses the cornstalk row to bring me Bill's bird.

"That's a handsome bird, Bill," I say as I hand it to him.

It's not long before several more tracks become visible. These birds are moving a bit faster through the deep snow, but it won't be long before they stop or flush. Pheasants just can't negotiate deep snow for long periods of time. Their legs and bodies just aren't built for plowing snow.

Near the end of the cornfield, each dog works an opening between cornstalk rows. Then both dogs simultaneously slam on point. The four of us form a half circle, leaving the birds only one open outlet to flush. And that's toward the cattail bog. With each step, I anticipate the flush at any moment. But I also know that it'll still come as a surprise. Looking over at Bill, I can see he has the same dilemma—never sure when there is going to be an explosion of wings.

The sound of wings breaks the tranquility of the landscape around us. The stalks and snow suddenly erupt and four pheasants launch skyward and then level off and fly toward the cattails. I manage to get off a quick shot and both dogs are immediately on the downed bird as it folds into the snow. I swing on the second rooster but hold up, knowing it's too far.

"Bill, did you shoot?" I ask.

"Yep, I have a rooster down several rows over on my side. I can see his tail sticking out of the snow."

"I'll get the dogs over, Bill."

"OK, thanks, but I don't think he's moving, Ben."

Two more unexpected roosters rocket out of the cover. We both watch them sail toward the woods, then dive into the cattail patch instead.

At the end of the cornfield the snow lies smooth as carpet over the low vegetation on the ground. But farther out the land dips downward and a long string of cattails stand silent like a column of soldiers. Their white helmets and brown swords stand up, seemingly ready to march. We head for the end of the column and I call the dogs back before we reach the cattails.

"Bill, we know three roosters flew into this high heavy cover. And I'm sure there are more birds hidden in the army of cattails. I'm certain the pheasants are not using the woods. The understory is just too open and the woods have no cover for them to hide in. So they have to be using the labyrinth of cattails or the cornfield, and we've already covered the cornfield."

Entering the maze of cattails, we lose sight of the dogs but hear them and see the cattails waving back and forth. In my mind I see the birds running around in circles trying to avoid the dogs and us. Ahead, several roosters sound the alarm of danger approaching. The dogs are no longer stalking, just racing around chasing birds in all directions.

Thinking out loud, I say to Bill, "These darn pheasants are going ruin my pointing dogs."

"Yeah, I know, Ben," he says with a loud laugh, "but they sure are having fun."

Just out of gun range, a drove of hens and roosters boils out of the far end of the cattail grove and flies back to the cornfield. Bill and I quicken our pace after seeing the cattails whipping back and forth, indicating that the dogs are on more birds in front of us.

Not far from where the cattails stop and the snow-covered grass begins the dogs become motionless and the army stands silent. With each slow rustling step we wait for the

There are many different ways to hunt pheasant, but for me a blanket of fresh fallen snow has no equal.

silence to be broken. Then ten, twenty, thirty big full-grown birds fill the crisp winter air.

Turning back and walking toward the hunting rig, I open the side-by-side. We both have our limit and every bird has a long tail and ivory spurs.

"There are many different ways to hunt pheasants," I say to Bill, "but for me a blanket of fresh fallen snow has no equal."

BOBWHITE QUAIL
(Northern)
Colinus virginianus

Size and Weight
  MALE
  length: 10-11"
  wingspan: 14-15"
  weight: 5-6 ounces

  FEMALE
  length: 9-11"
  wingspan: 14-15"
  weight: 5-6 ounces

BOBWHITE QUAIL

Hunting Bobwhite Quail in the Past

It wasn't many years ago that a southern quail hunter could find a productive place to hunt bobwhites by simply walking out his back door or calling a neighbor. But today much of the original southeastern bobwhite quail range is occupied by humans. City limits touch one another, suburban sprawl is widespread, miles of super highways flow across the countryside, concrete parking lots surround shopping malls, and the remaining rural agricultural areas are weed-free and clean as a whistle.

Modern quail hunting in the South is pretty much restricted to private invitation or fee hunting. Many plantations are now commercial operations that accommodate paying guests. Thankfully, there are still other geographical regions in which you can find this beloved bird.

Bobwhites are not new to me. Over the years I've made it a point to regularly hunt midwestern states that have good wild bobwhite quail populations.

West of the big river that divides the country, the landscape opens. Living in Montana, my direction of travel for bobwhite hunting is west to east. I know this road by the landmarks in my mind. It leads to all the old places and the new locations I plan to hunt for bobwhites. The mountains

Diet Icons for Bobwhite Quail

Habitat Icons forBobwhite Quail

of Montana fade into rolling hills of intermountain shrub grasslands, then into shortgrass prairie, and on to the mixed prairie of the Dakotas. Still miles from my destination, I turn and follow the Sandhills southeast. On this trip I'm not really sure of the exact areas I will hunt. My plan is to stay in a small town near several large blocks of public land, all in good bobwhite country.

The first two days I hunt a huge federal lands project surrounded by a large reservoir. Water is always close at hand for my pointing dogs and they have excellent results, moving numerous coveys of bobwhites both days. The third day I hunt several smaller areas of state land bordered by private agricultural holdings. As I put the dogs up for the day, a landowner, to my surprise, stops by.

Stepping out of the grain truck, he walks over, sticks out his hand for me to shake, and says, "I'm Frank Martin. I see you're from Montana, that's a long ways from here just to hunt quail. How did you do today?"

"Only fair," I say, "but it sure was a nice day to hunt."

He points to the area I had just walked, then asks if I hunted along the fencerow.

"Yes sir," I reply, "The dogs moved one small covey, but I never got a shot at them. They flew over the fence into the shocked cornfield. I wasn't sure if that was part of the public walk-in area, so I didn't follow the birds."

"That's my land," he said, "and the cornfield is part of the walk-in area. Before the hunting season started, I saw several coveys along the fence line while picking corn. If you have another day or two you can hunt my home place, if you like. I let a few friends from town hunt it, but they only go once or twice a season. This time of year they're after deer, and I don't allow any big game hunting. Last week there were two or three coveys along the lane between the shelterbelt."

I thank him and he draws the directions to his home place in the dirt.

"It's not far from here. Stop by and a have a cup of coffee before you go tomorrow and I'll show you the property lines and where to find the birds," he said.

I thank him again and wave goodbye as he climbs back into his truck.

The next morning I arrive early, not long after sunrise. The porch light is on and I can smell fresh coffee even before he opens the front door. His old black and white farm dog woofs as he ushers me in.

Frank Martin is a soft-spoken man who has lived on the home place all his life. His wife of fifty years passed away several years ago and their two daughters have moved on, having no interest in the farm. It was easy to tell he was lonely and liked company. After a couple of cups of coffee he shows me an aerial photo of the farm hanging on the kitchen wall. He points to the shelterbelt and the spots where he's seen quail recently. He doesn't pinpoint any precise locations, but I certainly thank him.

"Stop back after hunting and let me know how those fine dogs of yours did," he says.

"If I shoot a few quail, would you like some if I clean them for you?"

"Oh, I might take a couple if you have enough," he replied with a smile.

Not far from the house a covey of quail crosses the weedy lane in front of my hunting rig. I continue farther on and park next to the long shelterbelt Frank had indicated on the photograph. The whole area looks birdy.

After the hunt, I head back with the sun ablaze in the western sky. I stop at Frank's, give him a couple of cleaned birds, have a cup of hot coffee, and tell him the details of the great hunt the dogs and I had.

The sun has set when I finally stand to leave.

"Don't forget to come back next year," Frank says, closing the door.

Note: This trip was taken over ten years ago, and since then I've been back several times. Over the years a lot more land has been added for the public to hunt. Last year I hunted Kansas and Oklahoma to illustrate that it's still possible to have great hunting on land accessible to the public. The story at the end of this chapter describes that trip and how easy it is to use my method of "Building a Successful Bird Hunting Pyramid" to plan a successful trip.

Call 'em What You Like

Since childhood I have been fascinated with the different sounds that birds make. Two wonderful spinster ladies that lived across the country road from my family's home helped foster this interest. I owe them thanks for encouraging me at a very young age to be aware of the living world around me. One of the sounds I well remember from bright spring days was the loud whistle, bob-WHITE, bob-WHITE, bob-bob-WHITE. And each time I heard this delightful sound, I would try to seek it out and find the bird's breeding territory.

The male is famous for whistling its name. Though the bird's true name is the northern bobwhite quail, the most common and widely used name throughout the U.S. is bobwhite or bobwhite quail. Other names include bobs or just quail.

In Flight, in the Hand

Many game birds are characterized by the way they fly. For instance, teal whistle, dart, twist, and dodge. Bobwhites burst from cover like miniature bombshells that explode before your eyes. The wild bobwhite quail has great acceleration when flushed and the wing beats appear extremely rapid, giving the impression that it's one of the fastest upland game birds in North America. But bobwhites are not nearly as fast as they seem, which can affect the timing of shooters new to hunting the bird.

The average air speed of a bobwhite is about twenty to twenty-five miles per hour, although there is some evidence that the bird's initial burst and its maximum acceleration are twice its average speed. Whatever the speed, they are a tough little target. A large covey can rise with a disconcerting roar of wings, causing any hunter to shoot at the covey and not a single bird. Their diminutive size also makes it difficult to select an individual bird.

Bobwhites are limited to relatively short, straight flights, but the habitat in which they live plays a role in the distance traveled and the flight path. The average distance a bob-white travels is less than seventy-five yards, and if good cover is available it may be much shorter than that. But while hunting one riparian draw in a large grassland management area, I noticed the cover was such that the average covey traveled about a hundred yards. Much longer flights have been recorded. I believe the flight distance is primarily dictated by the surrounding habitat. This is why it's important to learn what types of escape cover quail like. The birds also require a wide-open window when flushing so they can fly in nearly all directions to escape.

A male bobwhite measures nine to eleven inches, with a wingspan of about fourteen inches. It's a plump-bodied little bird tipping the scales at five to six ounces. The male's most conspicuous markings are the white throat patch and the broad white stripe above the eye, which extends from the bill to the base of the head. Both white marking are out-lined by a blackish-brown border. The male's breast, back, tail, wings, rump, and tail are a mottled reddish-brown color. Starting below the breast, the belly and flanks are mainly white, with dark brown edgings giving the belly a beautiful distinctive look.

The male and female are so different in color that they can be identified in flight. The female has identical mark-ings to the male bobwhite, except in color. Her throat patch and eye stripe are a light buff yellow instead of bright white. And her overall color is much more subtle, with pale light browns and washed-out yellows replacing the clear white breast and belly of the male. The female is also a bit smaller.

Male bobwhite quail

There are actually twenty-one different races of northern bobwhite that occupy a vast region in North and Central America, although most are located south of the U.S. border. The birds cover such a large area, with different climates and vegetation, that their size and color can vary quite a bit according to local conditions. For our purposes, the most important race is the plains bobwhite quail, whose range covers many areas of public land in the U.S.

Northern Bobwhite Quail Distribution

At one time, the bobwhite had a wider distribution than the other five species of quail indigenous to North America. The northern bobwhite was originally found throughout the eastern, southern, and midwestern U.S. and much of Central America. In North America, its range extended from the coast of southern New Hampshire due west to the center of South Dakota and south to South Texas. This area covers over half the country. But not all of this region hosted a stable population. The north and west edges of the bobwhite's range are irregular, with a fluctuating population of birds largely dependent on the weather. Formerly, bobwhites lived in thirty-five contiguous states.

These prolific birds have also been introduced in several western states, but their numbers remain severely limited.

At its peak, bobwhite were dispersed over some 850 million acres of land, but today 80 percent of the people in the U.S. live within this region. Wild bobwhite quail may have less available living space these days than any North

American gallinaceous birds except the prairie chicken and sage grouse. Put another way, the bobwhite quail has probably lost more usable habitat than any game bird in the last twenty years. The reasons are simple: high human density, clean farm-ing practices, intensive graz-ing, more green-cut mead-ows, and other land-use practices that reduce or elim-

Distribution Map: The red line indicates historical range. There are many gaps within present range due to loss of habitat and human activity.

inate suitable habitat. The main problem facing bobwhite populations in most places across the country is the loss of habitat. All game birds need space and good permanent native cover in which to live.

One of the great changes in bobwhite hunting over the years has been the closing of private lands and the reduction of public shooting areas east of the Mississippi. But while the bobwhite's decline over a large area has certainly limited hunting in many places, the average guy can still find open lands populated with wild bobwhites. In the last two decades, quail hunting has shifted westward. The fact is, in some midwestern states additional lands are being added each year to accommodate public hunting for bobwhite quail.

A Bit of History

It didn't take long for bobwhite quail to greatly increase their range south and westward in the U.S. back in the glory days. These increases were primarily due to inadvertent habitat enhancement. Virgin forests were cleared to create small farms with openings for cultivated crops. One man could work only so much cropland, so fields were small and edges wide with lots of weedy cover. Today, this would be called sloppy farming, but it made great bobwhite habitat. The first stages of plant succession from cutover woods produced an abundance of quail along the eastern seaboard, starting in Massachusetts and extending throughout all the southern states.

By the mid-1800s the most desirable land in the interior for farming had been settled. This land-use change in the midwestern states greatly influenced the bobwhite quail population. Not only were forests cleared for agricultural lands, but miles and miles of tallgrass prairie and mixed prairie were broken for subsistence farming.

Most farms were small, usually a quarter or half section of land (a section of land is one square mile, or 640 acres), with different fields and crops surrounded by fenced-in edges. Dirt and gravel lanes followed section lines to individual farms, creating diverse cover on both sides of the roads. Hedgerows, windbreaks, and rock walls dotted the countryside. The bobwhite took advantage of these changes by expanding its range fivefold.

Behavior

I always think it's important for hunters to learn as much as possible about quail behavior. This isn't because hunting bobwhites is so difficult, but rather because so many hunters pursue these birds. With a limited amount of space open to public hunting, knowing every aspect of a bird's behavior and living requirements is an added advantage that most hunters forego. Time and time again I've witnessed hunters pursuing a game bird without a clue about its habits or habitat. You just don't hunt bobwhites the same way you hunt pheasants, or Gambel's quail like scaled quail. Every game bird uses its space differently throughout the year, and any gunner willing to take the time to learn as much as possible about that specific bird will have more success afield.

At the first sign of spring, the bobwhite covey slowly breaks up and pairing begins. This is when the male bobwhite begins making its most familiar call. But bobwhite quail have numerous other calls to communicate with one another, as well. The assembly call is used to bring a broken covey together. It is also used early morning and late evening to assure birds of the covey's whereabouts. Learning the assembly sound is particularly useful for the hunter after a covey has been broken up. It doesn't take birds long to start calling after being separated.

Food calls, alarm calls, and covey rise calls are all used at various times. Males call to their mates and help them find food during nesting. Both parents use calls to communicate with their brood during the rearing season. Bobwhites have a rich vocabulary for communicating with individual birds or the whole covey.

It is not certain whether bobwhites establish or defend a territory like many other birds. But whether they do or not the pair chooses a small unit of land with suitable habitat in which to raise their young. It has been fairly well documented that in some southern locations with good habitat both the female and the male will incubate and raise a brood. There is also evidence in some geographic regions that bobwhites can raise more than one brood, but latitude, habitat, and weather conditions certainly contribute to the outcome. Like other game birds, if the bobwhite hen happens to lose her nest during incubation she is very persisted about renesting.

In the bobwhite's northern range, breeding and nesting times are later than in the southern region. For example, in Kansas nesting begins around mid-April and is over by late August, whereas in the Deep South nesting starts much sooner and continues much later. Unlike game birds that have collective breeding grounds, called leks, paired game birds can spread out their nesting times over a longer period of time. Birds hatching over a longer timeframe have a greater chance of survival due to better weather conditions and more cover growth.

Nest building begins after breeding. Nesting sites are in areas where the ground is only partially covered, yet with dead grass or other herbaceous material providing overhead protection. Nests are generally located in open locations, not in thick woodlands or edges. Usually the hen lays an egg a day and at this time the nest is unattended. Early clutch numbers are from fourteen to sixteen eggs, but as the season progresses clutch sizes decrease.

Once the clutch of eggs is completed the adults begin the incubation period. The eggs hatch within a few hours of each other after incubating for three and a half weeks or so. After the last chick has hatched the parent leads the brood away from the nest. From building to the end of the incubation period, the nesting cycle lasts from forty-five to fifty-five days. This makes it possible in some locations for a bobwhite to renest at least three times if not successful. Nesting success hinges on a lot of different variables throughout the season and from area to area.

Good habitat and warm weather are important factors for the survival of young birds. During the first two to three weeks of a quail's life insects are the primary food source because the high protein they provide allows chicks to grow rapidly. The chicks soon develop voracious appetites, eating insects, but also greens, berries, fruits, and seeds when available. As the young birds grow and summer progresses, life becomes easier for the brood because available food is abundant and varied.

At sixteen weeks juveniles are full grown, strong flyers, and resemble their parents. Each covey still has a small home base, such as a thicket, within a much larger area, but this space also has other overlapping coveys that share feeding areas. Early fall is a time of disoriented movement for young birds, and the family units start to break up. By the time hunting season rolls around small family broods intermix and large groups of twenty birds or more feed, loaf, and roost together.

This break-up period is referred to as the "fall shuffle" and it's also common with other game birds. The birds' habits, food, and cover determine these movements. The shifts are also a means of relocating within the range to find protection and food in winter. These movements typically cover short distances. The normal range of a covey of bobwhite is about a quarter-mile, but birds of neighboring coveys often intermix. Even though a covey is tied to a small area, single birds that join another covey may travel much farther. A small number of birds have been known to travel several miles from their original home, but most mixing occurs in less than a square mile.

Most hunters think of a covey as a family group, but during the summer months adults with few chicks will join a larger group within the same range. Unsuccessful pairs also will join a covey. And two small coveys that share the same feeding grounds often join up. In fall, groups of quail of various ages may be found together. The interchange of birds among coveys continues throughout the hunting season. If a single covey is shot down to low numbers they will join another group, and small groups band together. Usually small coveys that combined during the fall will stay together throughout the winter.

Weather conditions are the primary factor for maintaining good numbers of birds going into the fall season with most game birds, but this is particularly true with bobwhite quail. As cold weather approaches, large groups divide to form smaller coveys of ten to fifteen birds. In spring, coveys are often larger than at any other season, but they seldom stay together for long periods There is also evidence that very few birds of a covey occupy the same home range from year to year because of neighboring coveys intermixing. Quail depend on numbers for survival. More eyes and more ears are helpful, and if an enemy takes one bird the group still survives.

Some coveys spend several days in one place and then another within a small area, especially if there is a division such as a road in their home territory. A bobwhite covey can become wild when subjected to hunting pressure and will move from one of their favorite places to another location within their home ground. In fact, a covey on the move will sometimes be found in an unusual location.

While hunting a wildlife management area in Kansas last year, I found three coveys close to a wide gravel road and not far from where I had parked. When flushed, none of the coveys crossed the road. But when I returned a couple of weeks later, the first covey of the same bunch I had hunted before flushed across the road into heavy cover. When I pursued this covey I found the other two coveys using the same area on the other side of the gravel road. The lesson I learned was that as the season progresses a covey will often shuffle to a new location within their range because of hunting pressure, habitat changes, or other factors like weather conditions. Exactly why these birds moved I will never know, but I suspect it was a food habitat change, not hunting pressure.

Living Requirements

The more you know about a particular game bird's ecology, the easier it is to identify or detect good cover types. It's also in the best interest of any sportsman to learn how, why, and when a game bird will use a particular cover. I take great pride in my ability to look over a block of land and figure out why a game bird should occupy that space. You don't have to be a wildlife biologist to have the ability to read good bird cover; all it takes is a little awareness in regard to each game bird's living requirements and behavior.

The more you know about a particular game bird's ecology, the easier it is to identify or detect good cover types.

So what are the living requirements for a bobwhite quail? First, the birds needs good living conditions year-round, and that entails having food, protective cover, a dusting location, loafing areas, and water available during the day. They also need suitable cover for roosting at night.

Bobwhites are mostly ground dwellers that eat seeds, fruits, greens, and insects. They consume a wide variety of foods in hundreds of combinations. This diversity in food is why the bird has such as wide distribution. Food for the bobwhite is an endless chain that gives it the health and strength to withstand the hardships of life, and it's vital every day of the year for the bird's existence.

Since the bobwhite is found over a large swath of the country, it is not surprising that its foods vary from one place to another. Singling out a bobwhite's favorite foods is impossible. Late in the hunting season in Kansas I found corn and milo used extensively when available. In nonagricultural holdings and CRP fields ragweed and other similar seeds were the bird's choice food.

The size of crop seeds or weed seeds plays an important part in the diet. Crop seeds like corn, soybeans, and milo can be consumed at a much faster rate than many small weed seeds. Western ragweed is one of the better wild weed seeds for quail because it's high in energy and larger in size than many other wild seeds. A large share of the quail's food is usually found in farm fields, which is why the bird is generally associated with the tillage of the land. In many public wildlife managements areas annual food plots and perennial foods are maintained to create outstanding quail habitat.

Even certain woodland types, such as shelterbelts, offer good food supplies. Mast is also eaten when available. No matter where you hunt bobwhite it's important to learn the birds' feeding habits and the kind of food locally available. One good way to do this is to take a crop sample from the first bird you shoot to determine what the bird is eating. Once you learn what a covey is feeding on, you can target specific areas during feeding time.

When you're hunting it may appear that food is always abundant, but that is simply not true. Food is usually abundant during the early part of the hunting season, but that doesn't mean the surplus will carry over until spring. Food diminishes throughout the winter and new vegetation and insects become critical by spring. Food also has to be available close to cover year-round, where the birds can use it. A healthy population of quail cannot be expected if food becomes scarce in some years. Wild seeds and agricultural crops produced every year close to good cover are the foods that sustain an abundance of quail. Lands purposely maintained year-round by state wildlife agencies for bobwhites are good examples of highly productive quail areas. Some CRP fields also are excellent quail hangouts if other habitat requirements are present.

Bobwhites don't need free water to drink, as they collect sufficient moisture from their food. They do congregate around surface water and will drink, but bobwhites satisfy

No matter where you hunt bobwhite it's important to learn the birds' feeding habits and the kind of food locally available. Take a crop sample from the first bird you shoot to determine what the bird is eating.

most of their water requirements from dew, seeds, insects, and succulent greens.

Bobwhites begin to feed around sunrise. They primarily feed on the edges and in openings in forests. A covey may go on foot toward a weed patch, crop field, or other food area where the birds will eat for an hour or two. Throughout their feeding period the birds may collect grit, which aids in digestion, but is not essential. After several hours the covey will retire to a sheltered place for their midday rest, called loafing covers. Birds are not very active throughout the day, although they do move about occasionally even when loafing and dusting.

Different cover types are used during midday throughout the season and in different weather conditions. All loafing cover types have one thing in common: an overhead canopy. But each one has a different density that controls thermal temperatures, which helps to cool or warm the area below. These dissimilar cover types help the quail maintain a normal body temperature at different times of year across its range. It's also important for the hunter to realize that there are different useable bobwhite loafing areas. Recognizing these different brushy sites can translate to success on midday hunts.

Coveys do move from place to place during the day, but as stated earlier, under normal circumstances daily movements are short. Even though bobwhites are mostly ground dwellers, there are times when a covey will get up and fly to a new location for reasons that remain a mystery. If disturbed, a covey will run or fly, taking the best escape route. During the day most activities take place under some type of cover or with cover very close at hand. Rarely will a single bird be in the open far from cover. Bobwhites return again to feeding places late in the day, usually about two hours before going to roost.

Bobwhites prefer to roost in relatively open cover without a canopy. The birds form a tight circle, with their tails pointing in and their heads out. This puts eyes and ears in every direction, ever alert for danger. Another advantage of being in a circle is that bodies are pressed together for mutual warmth during cold nights.

Good habitat differs from north to south and from region

Bobwhites and the Conservation Reserve Program

The dominant cover in most CRP fields is tall permanent grasses. Unfortunately, this type of cover is just not associated with good bobwhite habitat. The major shortfall for quail using most CRP fields is the lack of woody cover and the lack of open ground under the canopy of heavy cover.

Recent changes in the federal law have allowed woody cover such as shelterbelts and food plots in CRP fields, but this added value has been very slow to be implemented in many quail regions. Bobwhites will use CRP fields for some of their living requirements if the fields are adjacent to or within other habitat types they regularly utilize. I have hunted some CRP fields that had all the habitat requirements for bobwhite quail, but the best hunting was always along edges that had woody cover and open weedy patches.

to region. Experienced bobwhite hunters know that good quail cover has a certain "look." And that look is fairly consistent no matter when you hunt. This cover is not easy to define, but quality habitat for quail appears similar wherever the bird is found. Over half of the cover should be herbaceous food plants with plenty of low woody cover nearby. There is no real habitat model to describe the ideal quail habitat. When you find a covey of quail, take a good look at the surrounding cover and file it away in your memory.

Hunting Strategies

Bobwhites are highly prized by hunters and the seasons are generally long. For a traveling wingshooter from the northern part of the country, pursuing quail is a good way to extend the hunting season. And for the southern gentleman who wants to continue to hunt wild quail, it's just a matter of going west.

The traveling wingshooter should know how to recognize good bobwhite cover before taking a trip. Locating good hunting territory will then come easy. Without good cover, the territory just won't be productive. For me, recognizing high-quality bobwhite quail country comes from past observations and experiences. For the new bobwhite hunter, knowledge of the species and experiences in the field are the keys to finding birds.

I'm sure you've heard an experienced bird hunter describing good cover by saying something like, "The place I hunted today just looked birdy. I could tell as soon as we drove up." He might continue with something like, "My hunting partner examined the crop contents of the first few birds he shot and they were full of ragweed seeds. The birds had been feeding on ragweed in an area where the ground cover was thin enough for them to walk through, with some soil exposed. It was idle land full of weeds intermixed with woodlands. After hunting the singles we continued looking for other patches of ragweed. By ten o'clock we had moved three more coveys and every covey flushed to heavy woody cover."

You must start any search by learning about cover types and how birds use them. When I first view a new parcel of land I plan to hunt—I'm talking about a walk-in area or other lands open to the public—I first drive the perimeter,

Bobwhite Quail Ground Sign

The knowledge of signs on the ground left by bobwhite quail is very helpful in knowing that they are using an area to feed, roost, or loaf, and can save time in the field when looking for that species.

Tracks: look for tracks in sand, snow, mud, and dirt

Single droppings: look for single droppings along riparian draws

Roosting site droppings: family groups roost in circles, tail to tail, leaving many white and green droppings

Feathers: single feathers can be found in dusting areas and other openings

it at all possible, or any established roads that cut through. While driving, I look at the habitat and calculate whether or not it meets all the bird's seasonal needs. I note the type of cover and food sources to determine what time of day the birds use each in that particular area. I call this "scouting" and I do it with every new cover before deciding if it's worth hunting. If the requirements aren't there, I continue searching for new ground to hunt. When you're on the road with limited time to hunt, it doesn't make sense to waste time hunting unproductive country.

Bobwhite quail don't occupy all areas, even if they look good. But a good starting point is a place that has a windmill.

Sometimes I think the land looks birdy, but after walking a short time I realize the habitat just isn't conducive to holding a covey of quail. So I leave and look for better cover. Recognizing good quail country is a learning process, and the more time you spend afield, the easier it will be to find the bird's living quarters.

Some hunters will tell you bobwhites hold tight and seldom run. But the fact is that all game birds run; their legs are built for it and it's part of their escape anatomy. Running takes less energy than flying, and most critters use the least amount of energy possible so that they have a reserve to deal with immediate danger. A covey of birds knows that it is less vulnerable on the ground than in the air. And once a covey is flushed, its sole objective is to get together as soon as possible. It's an important survival tool.

When bobwhites flush they go in all directions, flying a short distance before looking for dense cover in which to hide. And don't forget the weather; a bob's behavior patterns change in different types of weather. Also take into account the time of year. Look for bird sign such as feathers, scratches in the earth (for food), droppings, and dusting places. If found, take into account how fresh they are. Remember, such sign is the calling card of birds living in the area.

Do I make mistakes when hunting a new piece of ground? Absolutely. But each time I do, I learn from my mistake. Keep in mind, figuring out how best to hunt a new piece of real estate is part of the fun of hunting, another piece of the puzzle.

Train yourself to think like a bobwhite. Quail don't wander aimlessly from place to place; rather, they establish a cruising radius or range. As mentioned earlier, the normal range of a covey is about a quarter-mile. Within that range, birds have a home base, a place much like our living room. They use this home base at different times of day, depending on the weather. While short-term weather does change the birds' daily routine, seasonal weather has the greatest effect on range movement. The birds may change their routine with the season, but their range will expand very little.

We tend to think in terms of one covey per range, but if the habitat contains abundant food and cover more than one covey will use the same area; such overlapping is common. But quail don't occupy all areas, even if they look good. Why some areas are used and not others isn't known. As with all kinds of hunting, no matter how well you think you know your quarry, the learning process still continues.

About Dogs

Dogs have been a part of my bobwhite hunting for many decades. The last time I hunted without a dog was on an outing with my grandfather when I was still too young to carry a shotgun. If I recall correctly, Grandfather used me as the bird dog. He talked about having pointing dogs, but I never saw one when growing up. Back then, the other folks I saw in the field were also walk-up quail hunters. But we were mainly pheasant hunters, and quail were only found occasionally.

Bobwhites can be hunted without a hunting dog, but most hunters that do so operate in cover they are very familiar with; they know exactly how the birds will react. The best time to hunt bobwhite quail without a dog is midday, when a covey is loafing or resting. With or without a dog, a hunter should always look for signs of birds feeding, roosting, or dusting. Feathers on the ground and tracks in the dust or sand are also helpful indicators. My advice for the lone hunter with no dog would be to choose small areas with thickets and to walk corners of fields and along fencerows. Go slowly and work spots that look birdy.

Hunting with a bird dog early or late in the day is the preferred method of many hunters, as quail are feeding or on the move and leaving scent behind. These hunters may have a point about the scent, but I disagree about the timing. A good dog can find bird scent throughout the day whether birds are moving or not, and birds never stay in one place very long anyway. Lofting areas are great places for dogs to work birds, and once you break a covey they're almost immediately on the move trying to get back together. I prefer hunting all game birds with dogs during most of the day, but by five o'clock I'm usually out of the field. The reason is that I don't like to break up a covey just before dark for the quails' sake. I've heard reports that a covey can get back together in a short period of time, but I've purposely stayed in the field and listened to quail still calling to get back together at dark.

For the traveling wingshooter who has a bird dog, hunting bobwhite quail alone is ideal. The next best scenario would be one traveling buddy. I've hunted a lot by myself and with other hunters, but I still prefer hunting bobwhites alone. I can put down as many dogs as I like and not worry if one of them

It's scary how much a hunter and his dog think alike.

makes a mistake. Bobwhite hunting alone with three or sometimes four dogs down is a passion of mine.

Dogs are immensely helpful for locating wild birds and for finding and retrieving downed birds. All of the flushing breeds are excellent at plowing through thickets and getting birds to flush. They work close in front of the gun and most are great at finding and fetching a small quail. Retrievers are excellent "combination" dogs for hunting pheasant and quail, and both birds are present in many areas.

Some pointing breeds have a reputation for hunting close and are excellent bobwhite hunters, although I prefer big-running pointing dogs for quail. Once a bobwhite covey is found and then flushed, pointers are excellent at finding singles. But remember, the secret is to give the birds

The best approach with pointing dogs is to walk slowly and keep noise to a minimum.

time to lay down scent before pursuing them after the flush. Then go slowly and let the pointer work all the cover.

The best approach with pointing dogs is to walk slowly and keep noise to a minimum. Noise puts a covey on alert faster than anything else because know it's an unfamiliar sound. Loud talking and other noises often cause a covey to flush even if it hasn't been hunted hard. Quail generally don't run far from sounds that are quiet and moving slowly. This is one of the main reasons hunting alone can be so effective. There is just a lot less noise. The more people in a hunting party and the more conversation, the less likely it is that the birds will stay put.

Where to Go

In the old days, hunters looking for quail usually headed to the Southeast. Today, the traveling wingshooter looking to hunt the best of bobwhite country should target the southern Midwest.

Over the past few years, hunting bobwhite quail in middle America has been outstanding thanks to many state and federal agencies creating and expanding public hunting areas for the average bird hunter to enjoy. A wide band starting in southern Nebraska, Kansas, and Oklahoma going through Texas to the Gulf of Mexico has thousands of areas open to the public to hunt this wonderful bird. Further east, southern Iowa, Illinois, and parts of Missouri also have public access to hunt bobwhite quail. But remember, non all these states or portions of the states have out-

Where populations are good in a certain region, public lands in these locations will also be good and these are the places you should concentrate on.

standing numbers every year. So it is important for the traveling wingshooter to key in on the areas that have an excellent quail population going into the fall season. Where populations are good, public lands will also be good.

Some states also contract private lands that are administered by game agencies that are open to the public. These areas have been a boon in opening up more land to hunt. All of the above states have excellent information about hunting public land. It is just a matter of taking the initiative and contacting each state to see what each has to offer.

Bobwhite Bonanza, Hunting Public Lands

I follow the designated road, pass an oil well thumping out a loud dull sound from a one-lung engine, and drive a quarter-mile farther on to park next to a windmill spinning with the stiff breeze out of the west.

The two dogs hit the ground running while I fumble with their beeper collars. After three blasts on the whistle Perk responds immediately, Winston reluctantly. For a muscular pointer, Perk has always been obedient. In fact, he has been one of the easiest dogs I've ever trained. At three years old he's field smart and knows the routine and likes to please. However, Winston, my second Brittany by that name, is a little more headstrong. Once out of the hunting rig he has no intention of wasting time getting a beeper collar on. It takes a little wrangling, but I get Winston fitted out and we're ready to go.

I unhook the barbwire gate, slip through, and close it. Then I drop two 5/8-ounce loads in my sweet little 28-gauge English side-by-side. My destination is the far off cottonwood trees, still a half mile in the distance.

The bottomland lies as flat as a pool table with pockets of cottonwood trees that follow the underground water corridor. Much of the understory is blue grama, buffalograss, and sand lovegrass, which fill the wide valley as far as the eye can see.

Over 150 years ago thousands of homesteaders traveled west in search of land. The settlers turned over the sandy soil, planted crops, and introduced the cottonwood tree. The new "sodbusters" struggled to hang on for decades before their hopes and dreams were blown away from the drought during the Dust Bowl days. But the cottonwoods thrived and the country was eventually converted back to grasslands.

Except for the cottonwoods, the landscape appears much the same as it has for centuries, a sea of mixed grass.

Looking at the cloudless sky, I'm thinking the country needs rain, not only to knock down the dust, but also to create better scenting conditions for the dogs. I guess I shouldn't complain; rains returned to most of this parched area during the spring and summer, making for excellent habitat conditions and substantially increasing the number of quail. I have hunted here in the past, and the country looks a lot more bird friendly this year. Except for a few clusters of prickly pear beneath my feet, there doesn't seem to be any sandburs present like before, either.

My sole reason for parking close to the riparian corridor is that the birds more than likely will be in the lower wash, out of the wind. Quail like the low sandy mounds strung along the high water mark, and the cottonwood trees give them good overhead protection. I know their routine begins not long after sunrise and by this time of day their feeding frenzy is about over.

Barely twenty minutes after leaving the hunting rig, while working along a sand dune that parallels the dry riverbed, Winston puts his nose high in the air and stops. I see him looking for me out of the corner of his eye. Perk is nowhere in sight, but after hearing the beeper sound the point mode he follows the same route I used and comes alongside and then freezes. Tail high, he crouches and stretches out low with his nose glued to the ground, apparently catching the scent.

I bring the side-by-side halfway up and look over the barrels, ready for the flush. I move two steps past Winston and the dry grass and leaves explode. One bobwhite comes straight up and I quickly shoulder the gun. Three birds go over my head. I take my eye off the first bird, swing on the closest quail overhead, and miss an easy shot. I turn back, hoping for a second shot, but to no avail. The rest of the covey disappears through the brush. Disgusted with myself, I never even mark the main covey down.

Sending the dogs in the general direction of the flushed birds is my only option. We make a couple of big circles and then I stand for some time so the dogs can work all the cover. Nothing happens, so I continue along the corridor to look for another covey. Just as we're leaving a single flushes off to the right, where the dogs were moments ago. So now I'm thinking the birds must be holding tight and the dogs aren't picking up any scent. Or maybe I'm not waiting long enough for the birds to put down some scent. Either way, I never cut a feather.

Walking along the sandy wash, I think about the different experiences I've had hunting bobwhites and how things have changed over the years for the average guy looking for a place to hunt quail.

Traditionally, the stronghold of the bobwhite was in the Southeast, but today most of the good bobwhite habitat there is managed by private plantations. And the cost of maintaining wild birds or raising and introducing liberated birds is enormous. So it's understandable that hunting on these preserves is by invitation only or comes with a hefty fee. Despite its limitations, it's still an enjoyable experience, just not one well suited to the average hunter. To find wild quail in publicly accessible areas today, you must head to the lower Midwest.

No matter where you hunt them, bobwhite quail are still a gentleman's bird and they lie well for a pointing dog. But the birds are not exactly the same the country over, nor are the techniques for hunting them. In the South, hunting from horseback or with mule-drawn wagons is the traditional plantation way to chase quail. I've had pleasant days afield this way, but I'd never choose it over hunting wild birds afoot with a couple of hard-charging pointing dogs in Middle America. And best of all, the latter experience is still out there for anyone who cares to go.

When walking this lovely country, time seems to stand still—until the beeper sounds the point mode again. Perk makes the next find. The main covey goes up, maybe twelve to fourteen birds. I shoot a single, then hold up to watch the covey. A straggler flushes and I take my eyes off the covey, but the lone quail follows his buddies and I mark a couple of birds down. Most of the quail scatter along the edge of the brushy sand dune. I take the last dead bird from Winston not far from the sound of traffic.

It's now late afternoon. I'm standing under a large concrete bridge, calling the dogs so we can return to the hunting rig while eighteen-wheelers thunder by overhead. Numerous concrete pillars span the two abutments of the bridge and the sandy, dry river corridor runs under it. It's all public land and access extends on both sides of the bridge.

Envision a huge map of the U.S. Now imagine two lines on the map, one extending from Los Angeles to Washington, D.C. and another from Portland to New Orleans. I'm standing where the two lines intersect in the southwest corner of Kansas on the last leg of a long bob-white quail trip, still a thousand miles from home.

For years, most outsiders considered this part of Kansas monotonous, with its short grass, sand-sage, and wooded riparian areas. To the uninitiated it appears to be nothing more than prairie, lacking any distinctive features. Though different than my home state's sagebrush flats, rolling foothills, and high mountains, the heartland of America has certain features that distinguish it from other ecosystems. Its beauty is in the land itself, which is covered by a canopy of open sky as clean and pure as when merchants and horse soldiers traveled the Cimarron Cutoff of the Santa Fe Trail, a shorter but more dangerous route between Old Franklin, Missouri, and Santa Fe, New Mexico.

In truth, I'm not here to see a subtle vista or follow the historic trail, even though I have a great appreciation for both. Some years ago I developed a step-by-step procedure by which the average person could hunt every game bird in North America. This trip is part of my quest to illustrate the effectiveness of this method, which I call Building a Successful Bird Hunting Pyramid.

The last time I hunted bobwhites on a similar swing through the heartland was years ago. And I must say, this latest trip has been more successful. The main reason is that more land is now open to the public than ever before. Today many states have started using hunter license fee dollars to purchase lands for recreational use, along with offering incentives to landowners to open up thousands of acres of private lands for hunting. Federal agencies have also played a role in developing public lands with the multiple-use concept in mind. So there is still plenty of land open for the average guy to hunt every upland game bird in North America. It's just a matter of doing a little homework to find out which species are abundant in a given year in a given region. In other words, you must go where the birds are, not where they were. Sometimes this means changing your plans to hunt a different species or a different location. And that certainly holds true when hunting bobwhite quail in Middle America.

Here's a look at how I use my Bird Hunting Pyramid to find the best hunting open to the general public. (See the next section for full details on using this method.)

First, I already live in outstanding bird hunting country. So why travel someplace else to hunt wild birds? The answer is simple: There's no place on Earth where you can hunt every species of upland game bird. Plus, I enjoy hunting different game birds each season. And hunting seasons are different for each species and from region to region, making it possible to extend the hunting season by hitting the road.

Within a couple of hours of home I can hunt half of the twenty major upland game species. For the rest, I have to plan a trip just like everyone else. Each year I try to hunt a variety of game birds, and several times I've hunted every upland game bird in North America in a single season.

Another factor in my decision is population dynamics. Simply put, in many parts of the country there is only one local species of game bird to hunt. Take ruffed grouse, for example. As their numbers are cyclical, every so often the ruffed grouse population plummets. During these years it's wise to go elsewhere to find good bird hunting.

My long-range plan for this season was to concentrate on hunting several species of game birds. Which species I would eventually hunt depended on how promising the numbers looked. And some bird seasons start in early September, while others, like quail, start much later, so the species you chose may determine how soon you start the step-by-step procedure.

This year the early projection of population numbers went something like this: Chukar and valley quail sounded excellent in key states. Pheasant, sharptails, Huns, and prairie chickens looked good in some areas, spotty in others. All three species of desert quail in well-known hunting grounds were down due to the lack of moisture, even though some less publicized looked good. Overall, western mountain grouse looked good. Bobwhite quail in several prairie states sounded promising. The only North American game bird species that looked dismal over a wide area was eastern ruffed grouse. I received no useful information on woodcock numbers.

Later quail reports from Oklahoma, Kansas, and Texas sounded as good or better than last year—and the previous year's hunting was outstanding in many areas. In fact, in these prairie states the projection for bobwhite quail looked to be the best in twenty years.

The rain had returned to most of the parched areas of Kansas during the spring and summer and most areas had excellent habitat conditions, which led to an increase in the bird population. Quail in Kansas had been down for several years, but this season might be a sleeper. Good possibility, I thought. Valley quail also looked very promising, but I'd hunted them for the two previous years.

After scrutinizing all this information, bobwhite quail soared to the top of my list. I hadn't hunted bobwhites in the Midwest for some time, and this looked to be the year to do it again. My intention was to hunt lands open to the public in Kansas or Oklahoma. Both states have done a great job in securing good places for anyone to hunt game birds.

My next move was to ask for more information from these two states. The Kansas Wildlife and Parks Department sent a complete information pack, which included a "Kansas Hunting Regulations Summary" and a hunting atlas of all the walk-in areas (WIHA) and state and federal public lands. They also sent a "Kansas Upland Bird Forecast" for each region.

Oklahoma's Department of Wildlife Conservation sent

their hunting guide, which included hunting regulations, season dates, public land descriptions operated by or in cooperation with the department, and other vital information to help the out-of-state hunter.

After pouring through this general information, I followed the Pyramid process and collected more specific information by communicating with every agency involved with hunting game birds. From this I was able to put together a diagram of where the best population densities existed in each state. Next it was time to decide which state to hunt. Most of the counties reporting good bobwhite numbers ran from the southern border of Nebraska through the center third of Kansas and down through western Oklahoma along the Texas line.

Within this region, Kansas appeared to be the best bet. The "Kansas Hunting Atlas" had a detailed map of each county showing every area open to public hunting, the number of acres, and the species available. Kansas has thousands of acres of walk-in areas and public lands open to hunting, and the quail season typically starts around mid-November and closes at the end of January. The dates for hunting seasons change a bit from year to year in many states, but by now I had the specific dates for this season.

Western Oklahoma also looked promising. The "Oklahoma Hunting Guide" listed the location of all public lands available to hunt across the state. Maps of these public hunting lands could be downloaded from their web site, wildlifedepartment.com, but after I printed several I realized that purchasing an Oklahoma Atlas & Gazetteer from DeLorme would be more helpful.

Oklahoma's quail season opens in mid-November and closes in mid-February. But it's important to know all the regulations because most public lands operated by, or in cooperation with, the wildlife department are closed during the first nine days of the deer gun season.

So after further study I decided to take the time to hunt both states. My quail trip was finalized by early October. I would hunt north-central Kansas for a couple of days and continue southward through other key counties. Then I'd take advantage of the reopening of Oklahoma's Wildlife Management Areas (WMAs) after the nine-day deer gun season. I reasoned that this would give the bobwhite quail a rest and that fewer hunters would be in the field after deer season. Finally, I'd work back through Kansas and hunt a few other counties on the way back home.

On most long trips I prefer to hunt alone so that I can keep a flexible schedule. I bring my own dogs, hunt a little more leisurely because of my age, kick a little gravel while visiting with other hunters and local folks, and poke around on side trips. On this trip my sole agenda was to concentrate on bobwhite quail, avoiding pheasants, and maybe take a day or two to size up a possible future hunt for lesser prairie chicken.

My hunting partner of many years, Buck, has a very similar hunting philosophy. He had no experience hunting bobwhites, so he left the schedule and places to hunt up to me.

We linked up and departed Montana early on the morning of November 27. With six Brittanys and two pointers, including one of Buck's, the plan was to stop that evening at a motel on US 80 in Nebraska, east of Cheyenne, Wyoming. My timing couldn't have been worse; a snowstorm blanketed southeastern Wyoming, so by early evening we were holed up in Cheyenne. Soon after, US 80 east was closed to traffic. More bad weather came in overnight and I awoke to find several inches of snow on the ground. We had no choice but to stay on in Cheyenne that day, finally leaving the next morning.

The roads in southern Nebraska and north-central Kansas were icy, but we slowly pressed on, hoping to get out of the white stuff farther south. But that didn't happen; reports of light snow extended below the Oklahoma line.

No matter how well you plan a trip, unforeseen weather can interrupt the schedule. So on most trips I try to stay flexible by keeping several possible hunting locations in mind. Thankfully, I did have an alternative plan this time around. Instead of hunting several northern counties in Kansas, we first we drove father to avoid the worst of the snow, which made for another long day of travel. That evening we stayed in a small motel in Pawnee County in south-central Kansas.

Pawnee County has fifty-six walk-in areas totaling more than twenty thousand acres, with both quail and pheasant present. To best use our time quail hunting we had to read the different habitats for each species, although some covers obviously overlapped. As quail prefer some high woody cover within their cruising range, I looked for areas with riparian cover, shelterbelts, hardwood corners, edges, or clusters of wooded areas.

Driving from place to place, I soon realized that many parcels were more rooster friendly than ideal quail habitat. To further save hunting time, instead of driving to each WIHA I searched my Kansas Atlas & Gazetteer for creek bottoms and other features more orientated to bobwhite quail. This helped a bit, but there's no substitute for seeing a WIHA firsthand. Each day we looked over several spots and then selected two or three areas to hunt. If other hunters were working a good bobwhite quail parcel we would move on but keep it in mind for later. But that didn't happen often. The truth is, we didn't have much competition hunting bobwhites because the majority of hunters we saw were after pheasants.

On the first day Buck and I hunted two walk-in areas, one late morning and the other early afternoon. I put three Brittanys down in several inches of snow.

It's dead calm and with snow on the ground I choose not to put beeper collars on the dogs. We follow a shelterbelt and within two hundred yards, Hershey, the old pro, makes the first find: a covey of bobwhite quail sitting tight under a plum thicket. The other two dogs are off to Hershey's right, and on seeing him they stop in their tracks.

I motion for Buck to walk slowly toward Hershey, then I move up and the covey explodes, heading to the thick shelterbelt. Two birds follow the tree line and both Buck and I collect our first quail. Not long after, the three dogs point a small bunch of quail in a brush pile on the other side of the windbreak. Buck kills another bird over this point, and I manage to scratch down a single on the way back to the hunting rig.

The afternoon hunt produces three more coveys of bob-whites. We're seeing plenty of birds, but I usually prefer not to hunt quail under such adverse weather conditions. Later we move forty miles south to spend the night in a small town in Kiowa County. This time my intention is to stay put for three or four days and hunt Kiowa and the other four counties surrounding it.

Most of the snow has melted off by the next morning, and scenting conditions are good. The dogs move four big coveys of bobwhites and two behave like they've never been hunted. In early afternoon I take the time to look over other walk-in areas for future hunts. Most are pheasant covers, but three large areas do have outstanding quail potential.

The next day I spend time photographing an acquaintance and his dogs. He and Buck are my models, along with his two outstanding German shorthaired pointers. Both the photo session and the bobwhite hunting are a success, but I'm looking forward to returning to our public lands hunt.

The next couple of days Buck and I hunt some WIHAs we found earlier. In the morning of the first day the dogs find one covey of bobwhite before pheasant mania takes over, and I tune up the dogs before they go completely nuts.

We leave the place, have lunch, and hunt two other small WIHAs. Both have bobwhites, without the "hassle" of pheasants. The next day Buck and I find four coveys of bobwhites, two of which we mark down for some outstanding dog work on singles.

Rain the following day forces us to catch up on other things as we make our way south.

It's early morning and the sky is bright over Oklahoma. My original plan is back on schedule. I'm meeting a good friend this morning who is staying on a private ranch, and I'll be photographing him and his dogs hunting the ranch.

There are times when the land offers much more than just a place to hunt, and the Selman Ranch is just such a place. The ranch's scenic beauty is wrapped in a fascinating history. The Cimarron River and Buffalo Creek have carved out a landscape unique to the surrounding country. Bison, indigenous peoples, settlers, and cowboys all spent time at Salt Springs along the Cimarron River. And the river's hospitality is still reflected in the eyes of the folks involved with the ranch today. It's a photographer's inspiration, a historian's dream, and a wildlife paradise.

After leaving the ranch, we move on to Oklahoma's public lands. For years, Oklahoma has been a leader in developing lands for hunting. In general, these Wildlife Management Areas (WMAs) are owned, licensed, leased, or under the management of the Wildlife Division. Most areas are large single blocks of land ranging in size from two thousand acres to upwards of thirty thousand acres. They're

There are times when the land offers much more than just a place to hunt. The Cimarron River has carved out a landscape unique to the surrounding country.

managed with many species of wildlife in mind and include features like watershed lakes, riparian zones, watering holes, and windmill sites. Food plots, cover, controlled grazing, burning, tree and shrub planting, and other habitat enhancement programs beneficial to wildlife are ongoing. Hunting these areas is a pleasure.

Buck and I spend the next four days hunting six different WMAs. I'm sure there are times where some areas are overwhelmed with hunters, but that certainly wasn't the case on our trip. Figuring out the best time to hunt public lands is an important part of the planning process. Factors include different hunting activities, seasonal considerations, holidays, the distance from population centers, fluctuations in bird numbers, and other small details.

I see no evidence of anyone having hunted recently as we drive along the gravel road that cuts through one large WMA. On one side, a half-mile of food plots and ragweed strips snake up a gradual incline with fingers of woody ravines.

"Buck, take a look," I say. "That's the best looking quail cover I've seen here so far. It has all the elements quail need to feed and roost, and there are hardwoods ravines where the birds can loaf during the day."

Buck slows down, studying the cover. "Should I pull off?" he asks.

"No, let's go farther," I answer. "There's a big building not far ahead with a white pickup truck parked in front. I believe it's a workstation. Let's see if anyone is around."

A man working on a John Deere tractor turns toward us as Buck pulls up alongside the pickup. Embroidered on his blue coveralls is a white patch that says, "Wildlife Technician." I walk over to the tractor and introduce myself.

I open the conversation by complimenting him on how well the area is managed for quail and then ask if anyone had recently hunted the food plots we just drove by.

"I haven't seen anyone hunting for a couple of days," he says. "There are birds there, but the food plots are so visible from the main road that they get hunted more often than other areas. But you sure are welcome to hunt it."

"Do you have any suggestion?"

"Let me get a map." He pulls a map from the pickup and lays it on the hood, drawing a large circle away from the main road. "In this area a couple of deer hunters reported seeing several coveys of bobwhite last weekend," he says. "I remember one of them saying the birds scared the heck out of him when they flushed. As far as I know, no one has hunted birds in the area we burned over a year ago. I'd work the grassy and weedy draws first and if you don't find them there hunt the adjacent hillsides planted with hardwood trees."

"What's the best way to get there?" I ask.

"Here, I'll show you on the map." Pointing the pencil, he instructs us, "Go back down the road and take the first right. Both sides are private land for a half-mile. Not far after the WMA boundary sign there's a pulloff. I'd start there and hunt the right side of the road to the lake and then work the other side back up. That's the area where those guys hunted deer. It may not look as good as the food plots, but there's a lot of good cover and it's full of ragweed."

"Thanks," I say, "we'll give it a try."

We drive to the pulloff, and there is no evidence of anyone having been there lately. I glance at my watch; it's after one o'clock.

Looking out the front window, I say, "Buck, there are times when things just look right. And this is one of them. We can walk this country and the cover is ideal for big-running dogs. I'm going to put down Perk, Winston, and Pat. We can go slowly, which will give us an opportunity to watch the dogs work all the cover.

The first find occurs in the burned-over area. The whole covey flushes to the wooded stands on the hill. After hunting singles, Buck and I work the dogs back and forth between the two covers and each time find a new covey feeding in one of the lower draws below the hill. I have no idea how many singles the dogs point in the wooded stands. But I do know the number of empty shells in my pocket is much greater than the number of birds in my vest.

Sometime after four o'clock we cross the border into western Kansas. I wake early the next morning, having agreed to hunt with an old acquaintance I ran into at the motel the previous evening. It's another good opportunity to photograph a new area, other hunters, and different pointing dogs—all on public lands. The photo session takes most of the day, but by late afternoon I manage to get away on my own with a couple of dogs.

The next two days Buck and I hunt together, but I don't want to return to the same area I had hunted the day before. Sometimes a place is so enchanting it calls for the silence of just one hunter.

Traveling north again, we cross over a long bridge. Looking down, I visualize what a raptor might see when hunting the lovely surroundings. Then my thoughts move to what I've overlooked while hunting this area. I settle back in the seat and envision water rushing down the corridor, a new beginning with the coming of spring.

Back in north-central Kansas, the snow is now gone and the weather has changed for the better. But our stop here is going to be shorter than I originally planned. Our first day of hunting here confirms the reports I'd received earlier that the bobwhite quail population is excellent. On the last morning Buck and I stop at a wonderful large wildlife area not far from the Nebraska line. I put down two different sets of dogs for a half hour each, and both groups find a covey of quail. Getting back in the pickup, I realize we're only a long day's drive from home.

Back in Montana, I'm next in line to pay for gas when the cashier asks me, "Where have you been, Ben? I haven't seen you for awhile."

"Hi, Paul. I was in Kansas and Oklahoma hunting bobwhite quail."

That's a long ways. How long have you been gone?"

"Three weeks to the day. And the odometer reads 3,930 miles," I say.

"I sure would like to hunt bobwhites sometime, but I'll bet the land's all locked up and you have to know somebody to get on."

"Not really. I hunted mostly public lands and there are a lot of acres to choose from," I explain.

"Which state was the best?"

"This year both were good, but next year may be different."

"Next year," the cashier says, smiling, "I think I'll go."

A fine pair of male bobwhite quail.

— PART TWO —
PLANNING THE HUNT

I'm lucky enough to live in a place that still has outstanding bird hunting, but I still travel to hunt. Because no place in North America has every species of game bird in one general location, any hunter who wants the experience of hunting them all has to travel at some point. But planning efficiently and effectively to make the hunt a success often seems overwhelming. The method I detail below changes all of that.

Building a Successful Bird Hunting Pyramid

Wherever I travel to bird hunt, my goal from beginning to end is to have fun. Planning the trip is an essential first step on the journey, and it may well be the most important building block for success. This step-by-step plan, along with all the detailed advice on where to collect information, will make the building process easy and enjoyable.

A successful bird hunting pyramid starts with a solid foundation. Each level has to be in place before you can continue moving toward your goal at the top. The challenge lies in narrowing your choices for building blocks and in making good decisions level by level. It's really quite simple, but to get the best results the pyramid has to be built from the bottom up.

The Pyramid
                    Birds
                 Being There
          Equipment • What to Bring
       Getting There • Accommodations
  Locations • Maps • Atlas • Gazetteer • Books
Public or Private Lands •Agency Listings • Dogs or Not
Bird Distribution • Select the Bird to Hunt • Select the States
The Right Approach to Gathering Info • Web • Write •E-mail •Call

How to Gather Information

Knowing how to collect the right information is the first tool for building a strong foundation in your bird hunting pyramid. Start by collect general information on where to hunt the bird you've chosen. Acquire information packets from the states that interest you. Surf the Internet, send an e-mail, write a letter, or call the specific fish and game agencies.

This material will include general information about bird hunting and regulations. It won't contain current information about bird numbers, population counts, habitat conditions, and the best areas to hunt. Your next step is to compile a list of questions that you can use later when talking to knowledgeable personnel in the fish and game agencies.

Using the Internet

Many hunters are now Internet-savvy. But even if you haven't used the Web to search for information before, it's not difficult to master. Using the Internet is now the fastest way to collect preliminary information about bird hunting from state fish and game agencies.

The Web is also a wonderful tool for gathering pertinent travel information. Any one of the many search engines will lead you to a wealth of great resources for every aspect of trip planning.

Writing a Letter or E-mail

Remember that when writing or e-mailing at this stage you are simply gathering information, not looking for a specific place to hunt. Be sure to make this clear in your introduction, and briefly list the exact information you want. Busy people in the outdoor information field are often barraged with questions, so the chances of getting a personal letter back are remote. Most of the information you receive will be general printed material.

You can also acquire this general information by calling the state fish and game agency. You'll usually be talking to a low-level employee at this point, so just ask for their standard information packet for bird hunters. Even if hunting information for the upcoming season is not in print yet, ask for last year's packet. Get on their mailing list so you can receive the new information when it's ready. Season dates are usually fairly similar year to year.

Review this information and prepare your questions before trying to contact higher-level personnel in the fish and game agencies for more specific information pertaining to your target species.

Using the General Information

The general information you collect from each state should give you a solid foundation for compiling pertinent questions for your more specific phone conversations.

Here are some things to consider:

1. Contact information for region or area offices or specific biologist.
2. State programs that provide access to private lands.
3. Publications for public lands to hunt, such as walk-in and sign-up areas.
4. State lands and refuges that allow hunting.
5. Helpful publications available for bird hunters, whether free or for a fee.
6. State maps available for bird hunting, whether free or for a fee.
7. Federal lands to hunt within the state borders.
8. The best time to call back about game bird population trends.
10. The general climate and typical weather changes throughout the hunting season.
11. The best time to hunt the specific species you've chosen.
12. The kind of habitat in which the birds live.
13. Inform them that you have a dog.
14. Ask any personal questions that may help you (e.g., Is it hard walking?).

After compiling the list, call the game agencies of the states that interest you. Always try to get through to an information specialist or, better yet, a game biologist, if available. These people are knowledgeable about their state's resources and can give you an excellent overview of hunting there.

Get the names and phone numbers of the regional biologists in the locations within the state that you plan to hunt. If a biologist isn't available in that area, ask for the game warden's phone number. And don't be afraid to ask to talk to these people. It's part of their job, so be persistent. If you are prepared for the calls and are frank and friendly, you'll often be pleasantly surprised by all the great information you'll receive.

The Right Approach to Calling

The reason for calling higher-level information officers and wildlife biologists is to collect current and specific information that will eventually help you determine the best place to hunt. So these phone calls are extremely important.

In my opinion, there's a right way and a wrong way to go about gathering this type of information, no matter whom you're talking to. Remember, the person you are talking to is usually busy with other work, so don't just ramble on. Use the list you prepared so that you can get the pertinent information you need quickly.

Be courteous, friendly, and to the point. Give the person your name and briefly explain why you're calling. Be specific

Making a Call

The best approach could be something like: "Hello, my name is John Smith. I live in Iowa, and I'm interested in hunting sharp-tailed grouse. I'm looking for information, and was wondering if I could ask you a few questions to help me locate some good general areas to hunt birds."

Then have suitable questions ready for the expert you're talking to. Don't just ask where the best places to hunt birds are in the state. That rarely nets a good answer. Instead, make sure it sounds like you've done your homework and that you're looking for help in finding a good starting point. Tell them you will call again when hunting season draws near.

with your questions. Have a notebook and pencil handy, along with maps of the state or area you're inquiring about. Take notes as you listen, and make sure to get the numbers of other information officers or biologists that work in the areas you are thinking about hunting.

Select the Bird You Plan to Hunt

There are more than twenty gallinaceous species of upland game bird in North America. Most are native, although the nonnative species have certainly contributed greatly to hunting across the continent. Nearly all upland game birds fall into one large group, the pheasant family (Phasianidae), which includes grouse, pheasants, quail, and partridge. The woodcock, of the sandpiper family (Scolpacidae), is also a game bird of the uplands.

I know there are a few devoted hunters who focus solely on one kind of game bird, but most hunters like traveling to new places to seek different species. Some regions have more than one species of game bird available. Just remember that when planning a trip it's better to keep the initial focus on a single species. Later on, you can consider secondary species, but don't let them get in the way of your main objective.

Selecting States

At this stage, it's important to select several states because you don't know where the best hunting is yet. Part One offers an overview of states that traditionally offer good hunting, but bird populations are fluid and may change significantly from year to year. [may want to restate this when entire book can be viewed] Search for states that have a reliable record of good bird hunting on public and private lands that are open to the average hunter.

Planning a Trip Using Population Densities

For all game birds population densities change periodically throughout the bird's range because of different land use practices, agricultural improvements and other factors that are detrimental to the species habitat. So population levels can decline or increase over a long period of time in some areas.

Numbers also fluctuate because of seasonal weather condition, and change population dynamics each year going into the fall hunting season. Also weather plays an important part in determining population numbers from one location to another. It's possible to have good hunting in one region of the state and poor bird numbers in another region. Population densities occur from different weather patterns over a large area.

Receiving pertinent information from wildlife agencies plays an important part in determining which state you plan to hunt. First it's important to get positive long-term populations counts in several areas you are considering to hunt in the fall. By doing this, you will have keyed into areas that has been good numbers of birds in the past. After receiving this information then it is essential to follow up later when more data becomes available from biologists and other wildlife personal in the field.

In some states field biologists do collect bird numbers by spring and call counts each year, which determines the rise or fall of a population in that location. With these numbers in hand they can be used to project the density of birds in that area for the fall the hunting season. Getting this information is important and should help to finalize the location you plan to hunt.

With bobwhite quail and pheasants it becomes more difficult to determine how the birds are doing once pair up. So very little information about population trends are studied early on other then spring road counts. But as late summer approaches, young quail coveys and family groups of pheasants become much more visible along gravel roads and other open areas. So field biologist and other people in the field can determine population trends for the upcoming hunting season.

Call Federal Agencies

Next, call all the federal agencies that oversee public lands in the states you selected. Ask to speak with the game biologists or information officers within these departments— national wildlife refuges, national forests or grasslands, bureau of land management, and tribal reservations. Refer back to your list of questions when calling these agencies. (See the fish and game directory for addresses, phone numbers, and Web sites.)

Choosing Locations to Hunt

Begin to focus on locations within the states you are considering about six months in advance of your tentative hunting timeframe. The final selection of where to hunt can only come from reviewing the current, accurate information

Licenses

In many states it's possible to purchase a hunting license over the phone, on the Internet, or by writing. In other states, it's just as easy to buy the license after you arrive. Each state has it's own licensing agenda for nonresidents.

Be aware of license fees, seasonal dates for each game bird, possession limits, land-use regulations, and other information pertinent to the bird hunter. Make sure you acquire all this information before you decide which state to hunt. Make it a point to completely read the hunting regulations.

about bird populations that you'll get as the season approaches. Department biologists working in the field collect this information. Information about population trends usually comes later in the season.

If bird populations have declined, adjust your plans so that you're hunting where the birds are, not where they used to be. Be prepared to change locations.

Make a new list of questions to ask regional information officers or biologists that includes the following elements:

1. Past population trends.
2. Population trends for the coming year, if any.
3. Call counts in the spring.
4. Weather trends during winter, spring, summer that may have affected this year's bird population.
5. Cover type—at the time of the call and during the hunting season.
6. Best times to hunt.
7. Private and public lands available to hunt in the area.
8. The names of businesses and sporting goods stores in the area that cater to hunters.
9. Add a few of your own questions, maybe something about any fee-hunting possibilities or local people that may be helpful with hunting information.

Start contacting personnel that deal with game bird management. You should be finished talking to the experts in the main office or headquarters. It's time to branch out and talk to the regional information officer or biologist, which will allow you to take advantage of accurate, specific information on population trends and densities. Talk to anyone with hands-on duties in the field, or at least someone who has regular contact with those in the field. This is when you'll really begin zeroing in on a place to hunt.

Ask for current information about bird numbers, population counts, habitat conditions, and the best general areas to hunt. And check on public and private land. If you ask a few questions in a polite manner, most of the information will flow freely.

Ask for names of local businesses that carter to bird hunters or other folks that could be of help. If this nets any local contacts, follow up with them immediately. This could be a sporting goods store, motel, or other local business.

Once you have as much of this information as you can gather, decide on the best state. But still consider several locations within that state. Set hunting dates to coincide with the most favorable weather conditions in that region.

As the trip draws near, call the most reliable contacts you previously made for the latest information. Then make the final decision about which state to hunt.

Locating Land to Hunt Before You Go
Public Lands

Some of the best hunting for many of our North American game birds can be had on public lands. Many states have thousands and thousands of acres of public land available and some actually have more public lands than they do private holdings. Maps from federal agencies will help you

Some of the best hunting can be on public lands because most are managed for that purpose.

identify public lands, and the DeLorme Atlas & Gazetteers and the Benchmark Map books are also helpful.

Private Lands

Many state wildlife agencies have established cooperative agreements with private landowners to provide free public hunting on private property and on isolated public land. For example, Kansas and South Dakota have very successful Walk-In Areas. Many other states now have, or are planning, such programs. The agencies usually provide maps for these areas. Always ask about these programs; they are a wonderful aid in finding land to hunt.

Many local Chambers of Commerce can be helpful in finding private places for traveling wingshooters to hunt.

They are also good about sending brochures that advertise businesses and have maps of the surrounding area. Local businesses such as motels and sporting goods stores may also help you find private lands to hunt. All of these places are interested in bringing hunting dollars into their community.

Some communities even provide a list of local farmers or ranchers who allow hunting. Some of these might ask a small trespass fee, but in most cases you receive good value for your money. This may even lead you to other private places to hunt.

Another way to find good hunting ground is through word of mouth from friends and acquaintances that may have hunted the location you plan to visit. Make some calls to folks you know who have hunted these places in past years. Call local newspaper and magazine columnists for information about where to hunt. I get a lot of phone calls like this, which is one of the reasons I'm writing this book. I want to make it easier for the traveler to find a good place to hunt.

Many county seats have plat maps available that show land ownership. This is public information. Once you have a chance to hunt or look over a specific area, identify likely bird hunting country and then check the plat maps. Don't call them; instead, visit the owner face-to-face at a reasonable time of day. Timing is extremely important. Never go too early in the morning or late in the evening.

When you first meet the landowner, whether he or she is working outside or at home, introduce yourself. Tell them where you live and what you do. If you have bird dog, mention it. Most farmers and ranchers like dogs, and respect people who have animals. Tell them you are hunting in the area for a few days, then ask if it's possible to hunt birds on their place. Be very polite no matter what the answer is.

Courtesy and an open, friendly attitude will get you everywhere. If they refuse you, thank them for their time anyway. You'll be surprised how helpful they can be in suggesting neighbors that allow hunting, or public lands you may not know about.

Bureau of Indian Affairs, Tribal Lands

A large percentage of Native Americans still live on reservations. But not all tribal lands permit hunting. After you select a location, the state wildlife agency can help you locate open tribal lands. In most cases, the best idea is to call the individual reservation directly for hunting information, because each usually has its own regulations. The DeLorme Atlas & Gazetteers and the Benchmark Maps usually list tribal recreational lands.

Tribal lands that are open to hunting require permit fees. In some places, both a state and tribal fee may be necessary. Other states don't force you to purchase a state license if you're hunting on tribal lands.

MAP SOURCES
Commercial Maps

At this time, some of the best maps you can own are the DeLorme Atlas & Gazetteers and/or the Benchmark Road and Recreation Atlases for the states you're considering. These maps have various scales from about 1:250,000 (1 inch represents 4 miles) to 1:500,000 (1 inch represents 8 miles).

These large books contain quadrangular maps that cover the entire state, and they're helpful for locating general areas you plan to hunt. They are also a great resource to have at hand when talking to personnel at the federal and state agencies.

They make it easy to find public lands and identify private holdings. Both map books have full-color maps that clearly show state and federal lands. The maps also list all the recreation sites, facilities, and outdoor activities available in the state. For the traveling wingshooter, owning one of these books is a must. These map books even list contact information for the Bureau of Land Management, U.S. Forest Service, U.S. Fish and Wildlife Service, Army Corps of Engineers, Bureau of Indian Affairs, Department of Tourism, and regional fish and game offices.

I don't go anywhere without these two big book maps.

The DeLorme Atlas & Gazetteers are available for all fifty states. At this time, the Benchmark Atlases are available for California, Oregon, Washington, Arizona, New Mexico, Utah, Nevada, and Idaho. They cost about twenty to twenty-five dollars a piece and are well worth buying. Both big map books are widely available at retailers or online. (See directory for contact information.)

Once you've decided which state to hunt, the Wingshooter's Guides from Wilderness Adventures Press are another good resource to check. These state-specific books detail upland bird and waterfowl hunting opportunities. At this time, guidebooks are available for Arizona, Idaho, Iowa, Kansas, Michigan, Minnesota, Montana, North Dakota, Oregon, South Dakota, Washington, and Wisconsin. Each book contains bird distribution maps and hunting and travel information by county. There is a wealth of information here for the states covered. (See directory for contact information.)

Public Maps

By now, you should have a state highway map and the hunting regulations maps. State highway maps are available from the tourism departments in each state. Some states send this map with their hunting regulations.

Many states like Kansas and Texas have even compiled free map booklets of public lands open to hunting, which include federal lands, state forests, state trust lands, and walk-in areas. Most state wildlife agencies list public hunting maps on their web sites.

BLM Maps

The Bureau of Land Management (BLM), an agency within the U.S. Department of the Interior, administers 261 million acres of America's public lands, located primarily in twelve western states. They produce the best maps for precisely locating private and public lands, indexed by quadrangles. They are also helpful in determining access to public lands.

These are topographic maps, also known as surface management maps, and have a scale of 1:100,000 (1 centimeter represents 1 kilometer; in inches, that's about 1 inch for every 1.58 miles). The maps are detailed and color-coded for public and private lands. They also show the topographical features.

You can call, write, or go online to order these maps, and it's often best to start by obtaining an index map showing what maps are available for the state. And BLM personnel can usually help you figure out which maps you need right over the phone if you know the county you're planning to visit. These maps cost about five dollars.

Forest Service Maps

The U.S. Forest Service administers millions of acres of public land in America's national forests and grasslands. They produce maps for each of these areas. The scale for most maps is 1:126,720 (1/2 inch represents 1 mile). These are excellent maps, and they usually show miles of the surrounding area. They are detailed and color-coded for federal, state, and private land. They also show township and section-line classification and include the index to geological survey topographic maps. Map costs are reasonable.

USGS Maps

Topographic maps from the United States Geological Survey (USGS) provide even more detail than BLM maps. These maps are on a scale of 1:24,000 (2 1/2 inches represents 1 mile). Now that's detail! These maps are often overkill for hunting upland game birds in open areas, but they come in handy in mountainous or heavily wooded country.

Getting the right maps can be tricky because they cover such a small area. Before you order a specific map, you'll need to request a catalog and index of the state you're interested in. Some sporting goods stores carry USGS maps of the areas around them.

U.S. Fish and Wildlife Service Maps

There are more than 475 national wildlife refuges in the U.S., at least one in every state. These cover 91 million acres and protect nearly every kind of wild animal native to the continent. Many of refuges allow limited upland bird hunting, and hunting can be excellent at times. After you select the state you plan to hunt, contact the state wildlife agency and ask if any national wildlife refuges offer bird hunting. All the refuges are listed with each state wildlife agency.

U.S. Army Corps of Engineers Maps

Many federal Army Corps of Engineers lands are listed and/or managed by state and other national agencies. The DeLorme Atlas & Gazetteers and the Benchmark Atlases show Army Corps of Engineers recreational lands.

Accommodations and Getting There

There are two general categories for accommodations: stationary and mobile. Stationary arrangements include renting a house, staying with a friend, or, most likely, moteling or hoteling it. Mobile accommodations include pulling a trailer, taking a pickup camper or motor home, or roughing it in a tent. Each type has advantages and disadvantages.

Camping

National, state, and private campgrounds are often good places for setting up camp. On many federal lands, you can camp almost anywhere. Camping is obviously cost efficient, and being on or near your prospective hunting grounds can make for a very good hunt because you spend less time in transit and more time actually hunting. There's nothing like getting far away from everyone else when hunting certain kinds of game birds. Like any other game, birds react unfavorably to a great deal of hunting pressure, and camping can give you an edge over hunters who must hunt closer to the city or town where they're staying.

The disadvantage to camping lies in having less basic comforts available. You can't come in from a hard day afield and relax in great style.

Getting information for camping is quite simple. All the federal agencies and state and provincial departments listed previously have information about campgrounds and camping rules. For public camping in individual states, write or call Chambers of Commerce, tourism offices, and fish and game departments. The DeLorme Atlas & Gazetteers and the Benchmark Map books also show campgrounds. The Internet is another great place to find camping information.

Moteling It

Most folks who travel to hunt birds choose a small-town motel or hotel for their accommodations. These facilities are the easiest to find, and many cater to hunters and their dogs. After a long day of hunting, there's nothing like a hot shower, a good meal at a cafe or restaurant, and a decent bed to sleep. And a hard-hunting dog appreciates these comforts, as well. But staying in town often means a long drive to your hunting grounds. On the other hand, if the bird hunting proves to be poor, you have the flexibility to quickly relocate to another town.

Getting information about staying in a motel is a matter of making a phone call or two. State tourism offices and local and county Chambers of Commence are excellent resources for accommodations.

There are many motel chains. One example is Best Western, which produces traveler's guides that list all their motels, services, and if dogs are allowed. Phone 1-800-WESTERN. If you are member, the American Automobile Association (AAA) has tour books that list motels, restaurants, local Chambers of Commence, recreation opportunities, and much more for each state. Also, using the Internet is an easy way to find accommodations throughout the United States and Canada. It's always nice to have a place to stay locked in before you leave home. (See directory for addresses and web sites.)

Driving

The smooth highways that crisscross America and the comfort of modern vehicles make driving a pleasure these days. Driving not only can make for a good hunting trip, it can also make for a good scenic vacation. No matter where you're going, allow yourself ample driving time so you aren't exhausted when you arrive. Driving to the place you plan to hunt can also give your body more time to adjust to things like time-zone changes and higher altitudes.

My preference is always to drive if at all possible. Nothing beats having your own hunting rig along, with all of your gear stowed in its normal place. I can take as many guns as I like, and since I have lots of hunting dogs I can carry as many as I see fit. Also, driving allows you to hunt

Nothing beats having your own hunting rig along and all the gear stowed in its normal place.

other places along the way to your final destination. But the biggest advantages are mobility and the ability to change plans quickly based on prevailing conditions.

Flying

Most hunters drive to good bird country, but sometimes flying is easier. It all depends on how far your destination is, the amount of gear you have to haul, and if you are traveling with dogs. Flying has some definite advantages. If you have limited time and must travel a long distance, this may be your only option. When I bird hunt in Alaska, I go by air. Even from Montana, Alaska represents four driving of days—each way. Although if you have a full month in which to hunt, driving would be well worth the time.

Long before you leave on your hunting trip make sure your dog is in good physical condition.

You'd be surprised at how close you can get to good bird country by flying. The place you've selected to hunt should be less than a half-day's drive from an airport. The downside of traveling by air is that you are restricted to a central location. If the bird hunting doesn't live up to your expectations, moving a significant distance is out of the question.

Flying does take a little more planning than driving. Make sure you can rent an off-road vehicle. Bird hunting is a rural sport, and no matter what species you hunt, gravel and dirt roads usually lead to the best areas. Also, when traveling by air, the amount of hunting gear you can bring is limited. And taking a dog or two is an added expense.

Airlines today have strict regulations on shipping firearms, ammunition, and gear. Many airlines allow only two checked pieces of luggage with a maximum of fifty pounds each. They may charge you extra for anything over that.

A security agent will ask you to open up your gun case. Make sure you take a roll of duct tape, and use it to tape the case shut after the inspection. This is to safeguard against the case popping open in transit. If you're carrying ammunition make sure it's stored separately from the gun.

Each airline has different rules for carrying dogs. Weather conditions, such as extreme cold or hot temperatures, may prevent you from taking your dog along. In fact, airlines can refuse a dog on any flight at any time, whether you are heading out to hunt or coming home.

Before you book a flight, make sure you have all the details from the airline's customer service department related to the amount of luggage, weight limits, transporting guns, ammo storage, coolers for taking game birds home, canine requirements, and check-in times.

Hunting Dogs

Whether you have a bird dog or not, this handbook will guide you through planning a trip to find different species of game birds. Many game birds can be hunted without dogs, although most bird hunters prefer hunting behind dogs. (Part 1 offers an overview of hunting with different breeds and hunting without a dog.)

Wingshooting Wisdom is not about finding the perfect breed of dog to hunt each game bird. It's about finding the best opportunities to hunt, no matter which dogs are used.

Today, the majority of upland gunners have a hunting dog or two, and the traveling hunter is more likely to have dog than not. Traveling with a dog is quite different from going alone, particularly as most bird dogs these days are also family pets.

Traveling With a Hunting Dog

Traveling without a dog means you can travel as you would on any other vacation. You can drive for hours, stop at any motel, and have meals whenever you want. You can take side trips and leave the vehicle unattended for hours. But traveling with a dog changes everything.

The more dogs one has, the more complicated traveling becomes. My hunting rig is equipped to carry eight or

Traveling with a dog changes everything. The more dogs one has the more complicated traveling becomes, but it's worth it.

twelve dogs, depending on the breed. I have a custom-designed fiberglass canine carrier mounted on the bed of my pickup. I've used the same carrier for almost thirty years and have modified it to fit six different pickups. One thing's for sure, it has hauled a lot of different dogs around the country. And it has been economical, durable, and safe and comfortable for the dogs.

My friend Tom Davis uses an aluminum dog trailer to carry his setters when traveling. Just like me, Tom makes sure his dogs are well cared for before anything else.

If you have only one dog, a good carrier is still essential. A standard air cargo dog crate is fine, and this is how most bird dogs are transported today. Make sure the crate is roomy enough, has a flat and comfortable surface, good ventilation away from exhaust fumes, and is securely fastened so it doesn't slide around when the vehicle is moving.

Traveling with dogs takes planning. Here are a few ideas I use that may be helpful, even if you have only one dog. Start with a consistent routine. While traveling, I keep my dogs on the same daily schedule they're used to. Feeding times at home are eight o'clock in the morning and again at five. Even if I change time zones, I stay on the old schedule until I arrive at my destination.

I take the dogs' everyday food and water pans. These are made of stainless steel and stack together, which makes them easy to transport. I pack several white plastic square buckets of their food. Taking water from home is also a good idea. But for the traveler there is plenty of bottled water available, and most drinking water throughout North America is safe. Changing to different water when traveling is not a big issue with me, as long as it comes from a bottle or clean tap. When exercising your dogs during the trip, give them a drink of fresh water using their own clean watering pan. Avoid having the dogs drink open standing water that appears foul or stagnant. Bad water can give a dog diarrhea, so I stay away from runoff ground water, puddles, and other open free water that may be contaminated.

I feed the dogs at the same time, with the same pans, the same food, and in the same amounts. If a dog refuses to eat when traveling I simply take the food away. Routine makes for a happy dog. They eat, rest, sleep, drink, exercise, and clean out at the same times they do at home. Believe me, this works great and saves a lot of hassle.

Besides my kennel dogs, I keep a couple of hunting house dogs, but they have the same routine as all the other dogs. Being house pets, I prefer to have them in the motel room, but I never leave them unattended. For safety reasons, I don't padlock the dog compartments on the truck when traveling, although I do when the vehicle is stationary.

Look for a motel before sunset. The ideal motel has parking available in front of the room, with easy access. I prefer a motel that has a large field adjacent to it or a good exercise area close by, like a park or a recreation area. After checking in, I go directly to the exercise area. I release two to four dogs at a time, depending on how secure the area is. A pan of water is available for the dogs during their exercise period.

Back at the motel, the dogs are fed in their kennel compartments before I tend to myself. And before retiring for the night I exercise the dogs again. I follow the same routine at first light; the dogs are fed their morning meal before I go to breakfast. Once on the road, the dogs are exercised around ten o'clock and again in early afternoon a couple of hours before I plan to arrive at the next motel. When traveling, exercising a dog twice a day is plenty.

I try to avoid public rest stops for exercising the dogs, as there's usually too much traffic, too many distractions, and too many other canine smells. I look for frontage roads that parallel the interstate or highway, preferably gravel roads that aren't used much. Many of these roads have woven-wire fencing on both sides, making them excellent places to exercise more than one dog at a time. Gravel pits, abandoned railroad tracks, state and federal lands, and traffic-free open areas are all good places to exercise dogs on the road.

After traveling the same routes year after year, I know where the dog-friendly motels are and have pinned down the good exercise locations.

Packing

Your travel plans will dictate what you need to take on a bird-hunting trip. The amount of time traveling and hunting, the climate, time of year, and type of travel all have to be considered. Traveling with a hunting partner and dogs also changes the scope of what to take. So every packing situation is different because no travel plan is the same. Still, I'm sure we all go through the same thing. What do I need?

Knowing what the overall climate and general weather patterns are for that time of year will help you figure out what clothes to pack. So get up-to-the-minute weather information and the long-range forecast for your destination. Today's forecasts are quite accurate, and it's well worth the time to check them out. Watching the Weather Channel on television, logging onto the Internet, reading the newspaper, and listening to the radio are all good ways to learn what the long-range forecasts are for the area you plan to hunt.

Packing for Travel

One nice thing about driving your own rig or if you plan on camping, is that most folks have all their gear ready to go at the drop of a hat, so packing is really not a problem. But make sure to write down a list of all the equipment you have with you before departing from home.

Flying takes a little extra planning because weight becomes an important element. You can take almost the same gear when flying commercially as when driving, but there are exceptions, such as aerosol cans, matches, and other combustible items. Contact the airline and ask what items are restricted for travel.

If you'll be taking a dog with you, check with the airlines for their animal policies and restrictions. One bit of advice, airline personnel are unaware of hunting-dog paraphernalia. So if you're taking an electronic collar or beeper collar, remove the batteries before packing them. I once had a beeper collar sound off in my luggage after I checked in at the airport terminal. Lucky for me, it was many years ago, before all the new security restrictions were in place.

You probably won't need most of the items that are restricted. My strategy is to take only the minimum amount of inner and outer clothing necessary. Hunting clothing it is now much lighter, more compact, and warmer than in years past. Choose lightweight, durable clothing, but don't sacrifice quality.

Boots are a different story, even when flying. Bird hunting is a walking sport, so good broken-in hunting boots are a necessity. I bring at least two pairs of good strong walking boots, with at least one waterproof pair.

For the traveler, it's important to remember that each game bird lives in a different habitat and terrain. Take into consideration the climate, time of year, and long-range weather forecast when you pack your hunting clothes.

Dress Wear

Here is my dress-code strategy for days afield near home or far away. Always dress for walking; keep the uniform loose for good movement.

Don't wear too many layers over your arms, as this hampers your ability to shoulder the gun properly. I wear a warm vest when it's cold, which leaves my arms free. I also wear synthetic stretch clothing underneath for good movement.

Most hunting trousers are made for comfort or protection, but few possess both qualities. I like light, strong pants for warm weather when hunting open country, and tough, lightweight, briar-resistant trousers for cold weather and heavy cover. But either style must fit loosely and provide comfortable movement when climbing hills or stepping high. Loose trousers are also cooler in warm weather. During cold weather, I wear a pair of synthetic long johns underneath. The light, form-fitting, stretchy underwear still gives me good movement when walking.

Pant lengths are on the short side, about one-third the way up the boot or three inches above the ground. Pants cut short and without cuffs may not be fashionable, but they're cooler, stay cleaner, and allow you to walk through cover more easily. I use the same trousers for wet or snowy weather, although I often slip on lightweight, waterproof chaps or bibs.

Upland bird hunting requires a lot of walking, so proper care of the feet is essential. Footwear can make or break a hunting trip, and to me it's the most important element of the hunting outfit. Good boots are going to cost some money, but they'll last a lot longer than a cheap pair. It's usually best to try boots on before buying them, although I've had good luck buying boots from mail-order catalogs, many of which have a bigger selection with more brands that you can find locally. If you do buy boots through the mail, don't hesitate to exchange or return them if the fit is uncomfortable.

I like hunting boots with moccasin-style toes. Other folks may find the round toes more comfortable. Whatever the case, find a good brand that fits well and stick with them. And there's no such thing as an all-purpose hunting boot; one pair of boots doesn't cut it for all hunting conditions.

My cold-weather hunting boots are full leather, insulated, and Gore-Tex. My warm-weather boots are full leather, as well, with a height of least twelve inches and a hard lug sole for walking in all kinds of terrain. If properly oiled and resoled occasionally, both pairs of boots will last a lifetime. I haven't had much luck with ultra-light boots. I'd rather have a tougher boot with a bit more weight to

Upland bird hunting requires a lot of walking. Good boots are essential. Breaking in a pair of boots is vital, so buy them long before hunting season starts.

clomp around in, one that gives my calves, ankles, and arches good support.

Breaking in a pair of boots is vital, so buy them long before hunting season starts. I wear new boots around the house for short intervals to get them ready for days afield.

One last thought about boots: Think about using boots dryers, portable and stationary. I own both types, and the portable model is part of my traveling gear. I use boot dryers on sweaty or wets boots after each day of hunting. It's like having an extra pair of boots—but a lot cheaper.

I'm a firm believer in wearing two pairs of socks. Whenever movement occurs, the two socks rub slightly against each other, which is easier on the skin. This helps prevent blisters and also absorbs additional moisture.

Hats are a matter of choice. A hat should provide protection for the entire face, but the primarily purpose is to shade the eyes. And to protect the ears in cold weather. Baseball-style hats are designed for cold or warm weather, and most are adjustable. I always insist on brightly colored hats when hunting with other folks, especially young, inexperienced hunters I don't know well.

Choosing a Shotgun

The kind of shotgun you select, its gauge, and even how it's choked are all personal choices that will depend on the type of shooting you intend to do, the targeted game bird, and how much money you wish to spend. If you pursue many different species of birds, along with other shooting activities, more than one shotgun may be in order. No one shotgun can fit every shooting occasion.

To become a good shot, your gun must fit you properly, and it takes practice to become reasonably skilled. The best way to keep your shooting skills honed is to shoot clay targets in the off-season. Planning a trip also includes practicing before the trip. It may mean the difference between bringing home birds and coming back empty handed.

But successful upland bird hunting requires more than just shooting. It also requires some knowledge of bird habits and habitat. Knowing what the birds are likely to do upon being flushed is invaluable. And the only way you can learn to shoot a particular species of game bird is through experience. Fully understanding any sport makes it easier and more enjoyable.

Because of all the walking involved, your shotgun should be fairly light. But the weight of the gun also depends on the size of the person carrying it. Flushing game birds don't give you much time to react, so a well-balanced gun is important for getting on target quickly. In general, the smaller and faster the game bird is, the lighter and quicker the shotgun should be.

Choosing a Gauge and Choke

Major shotgun gauges include 12, 16, 20, 28, and .410. The gauge of a shotgun (other than the .410, which is a caliber size) is determined by the number of lead balls, each fitting the barrel exactly, that add up to one pound.

Because of all the walking involved, your shotgun should be fairly light.

The 12-gauge remains the standard choice for most North American bird hunters. The 20-gauge is the next most popular, closely followed by the 28 and 16. Sporting clays have contributed to the revival in popularity of the lesser-used gauges. Due to its lack of power, the .410 is the least popular gauge.

To become a good shot, your gun must fit you properly, and it takes practice to become reasonably skilled.

The amount of choke determines the effective range of the shotgun on different types of game. The choke of a shotgun is classified according to the percentage of pellets that strike within a thirty-inch circle at forty yards. The exception is the .410, which is patterned at thirty yards.

The three most common chokes are: "full," "modified," and "improved cylinder." If the shotgun patterns 70 percent or more at the range specified above it's a full choke. The effective range of a full choke is thirty-five to fifty-five yards, depending on the game bird and shot size. If the shotgun patterns from 50 to 60 percent it's called modified. Its effective range is usually twenty-five to fifty yards. If it patterns around 45 to 50 percent it's called improved cylinder, with an effective range of just twenty to thirty yards.

Other chokes are useful in certain situations, as well. A cylinder bore patterns at about 30 to 40 percent. Skeet No. 1 is a little above cylinder bore. Skeet No. 2 varies between improved cylinder and modified.

Many shotguns now come with interchangeable choke tubes, and most existing guns can be retrofitted with tubes. So it's possible for one gun to provide the hunter with chokes for a variety of game birds and conditions.

Shot Size

Recommending a specific shot size, velocity, and shot load is an easy way to launch a loud debate among upland bird hunters. The important thing to remember is that killing

Shotguns

Many types of shotgun are available, and all have their place in the upland arena. Side-by-side double-barreled shotguns come with boxlock or sidelock actions. Both actions have a long tradition in bird hunting. Double-barreled shotguns also come in an over/under configuration. These types of double-barreled shotguns dominate the sporting scene related to some kinds of upland game birds.

Pump-action and semiautomatic shotguns are also popular throughout North America. Many bird hunters prefer them because of the number of shells they hold.

So take your pick. The most important thing is to become proficient with whatever shotgun you select.

power lies in the amount of shot put in a given place. The larger the shot, the better it retains its velocity and range. Smaller shot sizes create denser patterns, but they don't carry as far. Generally, the best shot size for upland game birds is the smallest size that allows sufficient penetration. The more shot that hits a game bird, the greater the chance of hitting a vital area.

Does a shotgun with a thirty-inch barrel shoot farther than one with a twenty-six-inch barrel using the same load? The answer is yes—but only by four inches.

For what it's worth, here is what I recommend.

SPECIES	SHOT SIZE
Pheasant	#7½ or #6 early season
	#6, #5 or #4 late season
Bobwhite Quail	#8 or #7½ all season

Other Hunting Gear

It's a good idea to wear a blaze-orange coat and vest when hunting, and many states require it during part or all of the season. Coats are for late season and cold weather; keep them loose and light.

What should you carry in a vest? Basically, just shotgun shells. The rest of the space is for carrying dead birds. And keep it light, with lots of good movement.

Every hunter should wear shooting glasses for protection. When traveling to hunt, glasses on second on my list of most important items, right behind hunting boots. For whatever reason, I seem to shoot better when wearing glasses. I prefer orange lenses because they collect light and improve object definition, such as a dark bird flying against a dark background.

I almost always wear shooting gloves, even in warm weather. I keep them thin and light, except in cold weather, when I switch to lightweight, Gore-Tex gloves.

I consider dog supplies as important as my personal hunting gear. I never go afield without a lanyard. It holds two whistles, a pair of long hemostats for removing thorns and porcupine quills, a comb, and small scissors for removing burrs and other unfriendly things that get into dog fur.

A complete dog first-aid kit should be close at hand at all times. Other important items include beeper collars, e-collars, leads, dog boots, pad toughener, water bottle, toenail clippers, and your dogs' health records.

Being There

It should go without saying that you need to be in good physical condition before a hunting trip. Start walking several miles a day, four or five times a week for a month before your trip. It doesn't have to be strenuous, although it needs to be active enough that you feel some improvement as time goes on. Be aware of elevation changes where you plan to hunt. A big change in elevation can affect your breathing during the first couple of days of hunting. Get plenty of sleep at night during your hunting endeavors. And drink plenty of water before, during, and after the hunt.

Being in good upland bird country is what it's all about.

It's your reward for the time you spent planning the trip. Once you reach good hunting grounds, take some time to look over the whole area. No matter where you go, it's to your advantage to drive back roads and look for potential cover. It's well worth the time, and it will pay big dividends on future hunts to the region.

Take your time and talk to folks that live in the area. This could be at a local cafe, general store, sporting goods store, gas station, farm, or ranch. Kicking a little dirt with local folks can open doors to outstanding hunting on public and private lands no matter what part of North America you're visiting.

With a Dog

I certainly hope that any dog you take on a hunting trip is in good physical condition and able to hunt safely and effectively for the number of days you have planned. Without saying, the best performing dogs are those at the top of their game. Dogs need off-season conditioning just like hunters do.

It's a good idea to give your dog a bit more food on a hunting trip if he's working particularly hard. And like people, hard-working dogs should get lots of rest. Have ample water available for your dog when in the field. Water is the key to keeping a dog running hard, and it helps scenting ability. Make sure you have a warm, comfortable place for your dog to rest a night. On the road or in the field, care of your dog comes first.

Caring for Game Birds

All game bird make delicious eating if taken care of properly. Some hunters like to hang or refrigerate the birds for several days before cooking them, others prefer to cook or freeze birds as quickly as possible. Either way, a good game-bird meal begins with proper field care.

In the Field

Game birds should be cooled down gradually. If the weather is warm or hot, don't leave birds in the sun or in a hot game bag for long periods. Put them in a cool location and, if at all possible, let air circulate around them. It's usually best to field dress the birds after the day's hunt. Then hang, refrigerate, or freeze them before picking or skinning. Yes, I do freeze game birds with the feathers on. I believe it prevents the birds from drying out or getting freezer burn. You can also skin the birds at the same time you gut them in the field, refrigerating or freezing them depending on your philosophy and travel plans.

Preparing Birds for Travel

Here's how I handle birds on a hunting trip. Each day after hunting, I gut the birds, leaving the feathers on. If it's cool I hang them. If it's warm I wrap each bird in newspaper and place it in a cooler with plastic ice packs at the bottom. The birds stay dry and the newspaper helps insulate the cooler.

When traveling by air, I take the cooler full of birds with me. If the birds have been hung, I wrap them in news-

Vehicles in the Field

Most of my bird hunting takes place far off the main gravel roads, so I use a reliable vehicle that can traverse the backcountry without getting into difficulty. Sometimes this means driving on two-rut dirt roads, section-line roads, or even tractor lanes used only for planting and harvest. In walk-in and wildlife management areas park in designated zones. I stick to the landowner's established roads and never create new trails. I do the same on public land, staying only on designated roads.

Most trucks and SUVs have four-wheel drive in high and low ranges. These are wonderful hunting vehicles, but just because your rig is the ideal hunting buggy around home doesn't mean it can go anywhere. Tires are one important consideration. Some are better for sandy soil, other for "gumbo" or rocky terrain.

Driving down into a coulee may seem easy enough, but a sudden rain or snowstorm could make getting back out difficult to impossible. A rainstorm a day before a hunting trip should put you on guard. Different kinds of soil absorb and hold water differently. After a hard rain, gumbo may quickly develop on previously hard-packed roads, while sandy terrain often has deep ruts that can be difficult to clear.

Jacks, come-along, winches, and other accessories can sometimes get you out of a backcountry predicament when help is many miles away. If do carry such equipment, think of it only in terms of an unforeseen emergency, not as an excuse to take unnecessary chances. I always have a good shovel in my vehicle, and these days, having a cell phone along isn't a bad idea, either. One last word about hunting off the beaten path: Make sure you have an extra set of keys for your hunting partner. I also like to duct-tape an extra key to the undercarriage of hunting rig, so I never have to worry about being locked out or losing a key.

paper and place them in a cardboard box before shipping.

If I'm on an extended driving trip I keep the birds in a cooler for several days, then find a way to keep them frozen. Once home, I place each bird in a Ziploc bag and freeze it.

Have ample water available for your dog when in the field. Water is the key to keeping a dog running hard.

Preparing Birds for the Taxidermist

A taxidermist can preserve your wingshooting memories for years to come. It's important to find a taxidermist whose work is pleasing to your eye, as styles often differ. Ask around about taxidermists near home, or contact the local Chamber of Commence or a sporting goods store if you want to find a taxidermist while on a long trip. Get some references or go see his work. The Internet is also a great resource. Simply go to one of the major search engines and type in what you're looking for. Select a few likely candidates, and request testimonials or pictures of his work.

Mature birds make the best mounts. Select a bird that isn't too damaged and blot any leaking fluids, although a bird that has some blood on it can be taken care of by a taxidermist. Smooth the feathers and let the bird cool down, then wrap it in something soft. A paper towel or newspaper works fine. Just make sure the feathers aren't ruffled.

After the day's hunt, put the bird in a Ziploc bag and place it in a cooler or freeze it. Once frozen, the bird can last several months before being worked on. If you need to ship the bird, call your taxidermist for instructions.

Directory for Information Gathering

State Fish and Game Departments

Alabama Division of Game & Fish
64 N Union Street
[missing town, state, zip]
334-242-3469
www.denr.state.al.us/agfd

Alaska Department of Fish & Game
P.O. Box 25526
Juneau, AK 99802
907-465-4100
www.state.ak.us/adfg

Arizona Game & Fish Department
2221 W. Greenway Road
Phoenix, AZ 85023
602-942-3000
www.state.azgfd.com

Arkansas Game & Fish Commission
2 Natural Resources Drive
Little Rock, AR 72205
501-223-6300
www.agfc.com

California Department of Fish & Game
1416 9th Street
Sacramento, CA 95814
916-653-7664
www.dfg.ca.gov

Colorado Division of Wildlife
6060 Broadway
Denver, CO 80216
303-29701192
www.wildlife.state.co.us

Connecticut Department of Environmental
Protection
79 Elm Street
Hartford, CT 06106
860-424-3011
www.dep.state.ct.us

Delaware Division of Fish & Wildlife
89 Kings Highway
Dover, DE 19901
302-739-5297
www.dnrec.state.de.us

Florida Fish & Wildlife Cons. Commission
620 S Meridian Street
Tallahassee, FL 32399
850-922-4330
www.floridacoserservation.org

Georgia Wildlife Resources Division
2111 US 278 SE
Social Circle, GA 30025
770-918-6416
www.georgiawildlife.com

Idaho Fish & Game Department
P.O. Box 25
600 S Walnut Street
Boise, ID 83707
208-334-3700
ww.state.id.us/fishgame

Illinois Department of Natural Resources
1 Natural Resources Way
Springfield, IL 62702
217-782-6424
www.dnr.state.il.us

Indiana Division of Fish & Game
402 W. Washington Street
Room W 273
Indianapolis, IN 46204
317-232-4080
www.wildlife.in gov

Iowa Department of Natural Resources
502 E. 9th
Wallace State Office Bldg.
Des Moines, IA 50319
515-281-5918
www.state.ia.us/dnr

Kansas Department of Wildlife & Parks
512 SE 25th Avenue
Pratt, KS 67124
316-672-5911
www.kdwp.state.ks.us

Kentucky Department of Fish & Wildlife
1 Game Farm Road
Frankfurt, KY 40601
1-800-858-1549
www.kdfwr.state.ky.us

Maine Dept. of Inland Fisheries & Wildlife
41 State House Station
284 State Street
Augusta, ME 04333
207-287-8000
www.state.me.us/ifw

Maryland Dept. of Natural Resources
580 Taylor Avenue
Wildlife & Heritage Division
Annapolis, MD 21401
410-260-8540
www.dnr.state.md.us

Massachusetts Dept. of Fish & Wildlife
251 Causeway Street
Suite 400
Boston, MA 02114
617-626-1590
www.state.ma.us/dfwele

Michigan Department of Natural Res.
P.O. Box 30444
Wildlife Division
Lansing, MI 48909
517-373-1263
www.dnr.state.mi.us

Minnesota Department of Natural
Resources
500 Lafayette Road N
St. Paul, MN 55155
651-296-6157
www.dnr.state.mn.us

Mississippi Department of Wildlife,
Fisheries & Parks
1505 Eastover Drive
Jackson, MS 39211
601-432-2400
www.mdwfp.com

Missouri Department of Conservation
2901 W. Truman Boulevard
P.O. Box 180
Jefferson City, MO 65109
573-751-4115
www.conservation.state.mo.us

Montana Department of Fish, Wildlife &
Parks
1420 E. 6th Avenue
Helena, MT 59620
406-444-2950
www.fwp.state.mt.us

Nebraska Game & Parks Commission
2200 N 33rd Street
Lincoln, NE 68503
402-471-0641
www.ngpc.state.ne.us

Nevada Division of Wildlife
1100 Valley Road
Reno, NV 89512
775-688-1500
www.nevadadivisionofwildlife.org

New Hampshire Fish & Game
Department
Public Affairs Division
2 Hazen Drive
Concord, NH 03301
603-271-2461
www.wildlife.state.nh.us

New Jersey Division of Fish & Wildlife
P.O. Box 400
Trenton, NJ 08625
609-292-2965
www.state.nj.us/dep/fgw

New Mexico Game & Fish Department
P.O. Box 25112
Santa Fe, NM 87504
505-827-7911
www.gmfsh.state.nm.us

New York Department of Environmental
Conservation
625 Broadway
Albany, NY 12233
518-402-8845
www.dec.state.ny.us

North Carolina Wildlife Resources
Commission
1722 Mail Service Center
Division of Wildlife Management
Raleigh, NC 27699
919-733-7291
www.ncwildlife.org

North Dakota State Game & Fish Dept.
100 N Bismark Expressway
Bismark, ND 58501
701-328-6300
www.state.nd.us/gnf

Ohio Division of Wildlife
1840 Belcher Drive
Columbus, OH 43224
614-265-6300
www.dnr.state.oh.us/wildlife

Oklahoma Dept. of Wildlife Conservation
P.O. Box 53465
Wildlife Division
Oklahoma City, OK 73152
406-521-3851
ww.wildlifedepartment.com

Oregon Department of Fish & Game
P.O. Box 59
2501 SW First Avenue
Portland, OR 97207
503-872-5268
www.dfwstate.or.us

Pennsylvania Game Commission
2001 Elmerton Avenue
Harrisburg, PA 17110
717-784-250
www.pgc.state.pa.us

Rhode Island Division of Fish & Game
4808 Tower Hill Road
Wakefield, RI 02879
401-789-3094
www.state.ri.us/ dem

South Carolina Department of Natural
Resources
Rembert C Dennis Building
P.O. Box 167
Game and Fish Department
Columbia, SC 29202
803-734-3888

South Dakota Game, Fish & Parks
523 E. Capitol Avenue
Pierre, SD 57501
605-773-3485
www.state.sd.us/gfp

Tennessee Wildlife Resources Agency
Ellington Agricultural Center
P.O. Box 40747
Nashville, TN 37204
615-781-6610
www.state.tn/twra

Texas Parks & Wildlife Department
4200 Smith School Road
Austin, TX 78744
1-800-792-1112
www.tpwd.state.tx.us

Utah Department of Natural Resources
1594 W North Temple
Division of Wildlife Resources
Salt Lake City, UT 84114
801-538-4700
www.wildlife.utah.gov

Vermont Fish & Wildlife Department
103 S Main Street
10 S. Building
Waterbury, VT 05671
802-241-3700
www.anr.state.vt.us

Virginia Department of Game & Inland
Fisheries
4010 W Broad Street
Richmond, VA 23230
804-367-1000
www.dgif.state.va.us

Washington Department of Fish &
Wildlife
600 Capitol Way N.
Olympia, WA 98501
360-902-2200
www.wa.gov/wdfw

West Virginia Division of Natural
Resources
1900 Kanawha Boulevard E.
State Capital Complex Bldg. 3
Charleston, WV 25305
304-558-2758
www.dnr.state.wv.us

Wisconsin Department of Natural
Resources
191 S. Webster Street
Madison, WI 53707
608-266-2621
www.dnr.state.wi.us

Wyoming Game & Fish Department
5400 Bishop Boulevard
Cheyenne, WY 82006
307-777-4600
www.gf.state.wy.us

Map Sources

Commercial Maps:

DeLorme Mapping Company
Two DeLorme Drive
P.O. Box 298
Yarmouth, ME 04096
1-800-452-5931 or 207-865-417
www.delorme.com
The DeLorme Atlas & Gazetteer, all fifty
states: www delorme.com

Benchmark Maps
Map Link
30 South La Patera Lane, Unit 5
Goleta, CA 93117
805-692-6777
www maplink.com
Benchmark Maps, available for western
states: www.benchmark map.com

Wilderness Adventures, Inc.
P.O. Box 38
Montaque, MI 49437-0038

Public Map Sources:

BLM Maps

U.S. Bureau of Land Management
Office of Public Affairs
1849 C Street Room406-LS
Washington, DC 20240
202-452-5125
For regional offices, visit: www.blm.gov

Forest Service Maps

Washington Office
Sydney R. Yates Building
201 14th Street SW
Washington DC 20024
202-205-8333
    (Mailing Address)
    P.O. Box 96090
    Washington, DC 20090-6090
For regional offices, visit: www.fs fed.us

USGS Maps

U.S. Geological Survey
Information Services
P.O. Box 25286
Denver, CO 80225
888-ASK-USGS
inforservices@usgs.gov

Maps, all states: www.50state.com

Internet Sites

State Fish and Wildlife Agencies, all states: www.dfw.state.or.us/ODFWhtml/MiscFiles/StateLink2.html

U.S. Fish & Wildlife Service: ww.fws.gov Region Offices: www.dfw.state.com

Bureau of Land Management: www.blm.gov

U.S. Army Corps of Engineers: Search for hunting at www.usace.army.mil

Forest Service, national forests and grasslands: www.fs fed.us/recreation

U.S. Geological Survey: www.usgs.gov

State information about destinations & misc. websites

www.tourstates.com

Specific state tourism information: www.2chambers.com

National directory for state and town facilities: www.travel.com

Traveling information for dogs: www.dogpile.com

Pet-friendly accommodations: www.petswelcome.com or www.peton-thego.com

Vet locations: www.veterinariansdirectory.com or www.americanveterinariansdirectory.com

Camping: www.CampUSA.com or www.camping.usa.com or www.the.campground.network.com